Adult Coloring Book

Stress Relieving Patterns

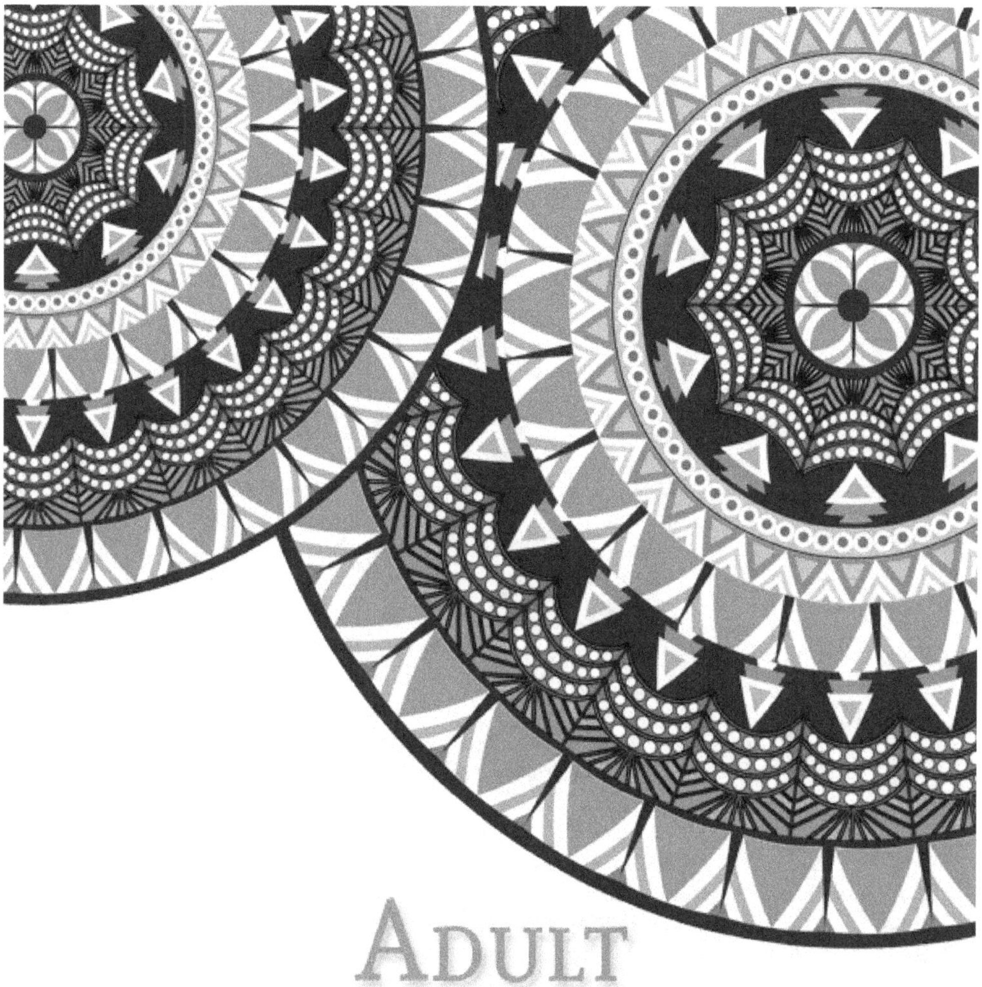

ADULT COLORING BOOK

Stress Relieving Patterns

Vol. 1

V ART™

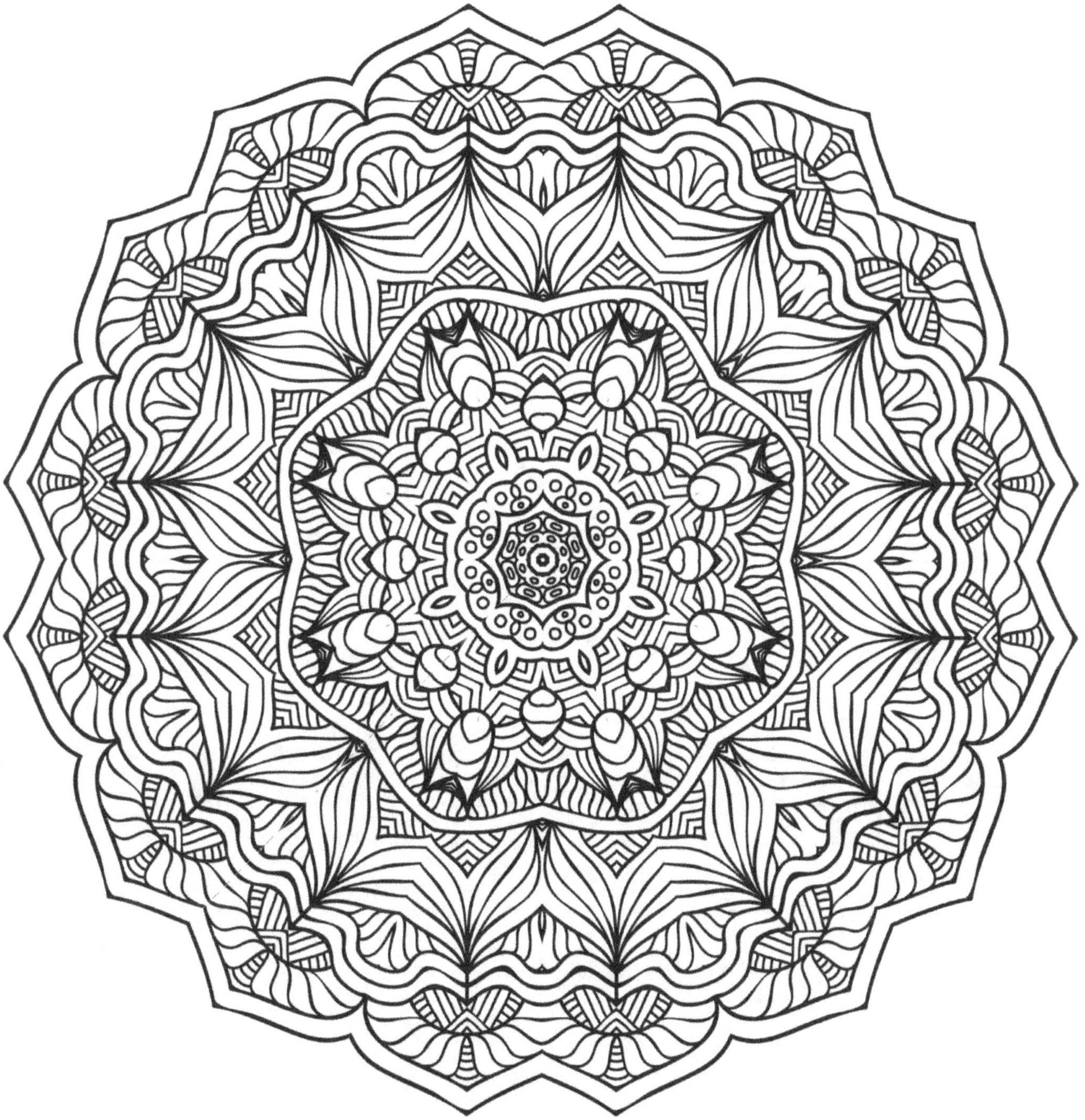

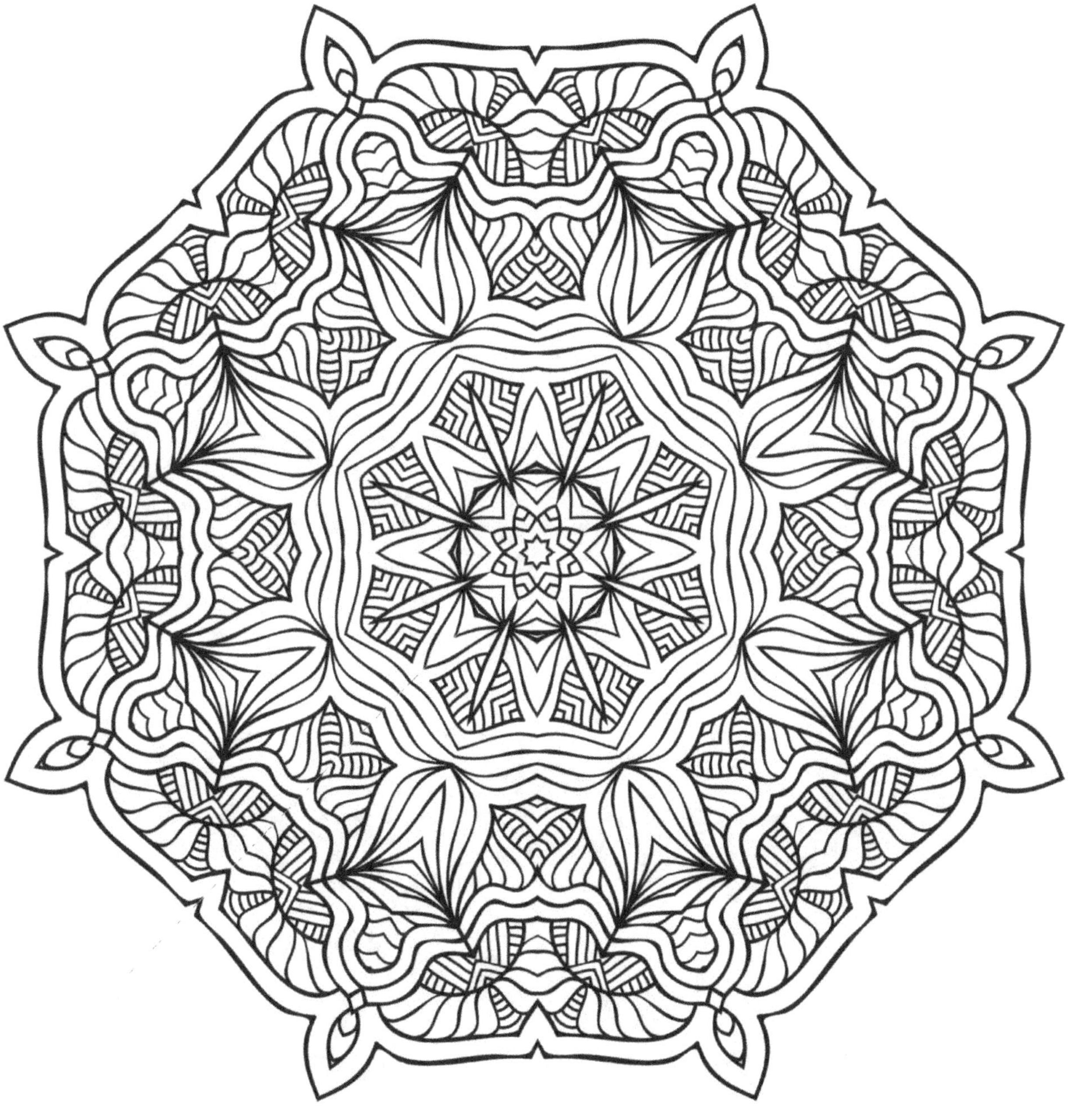

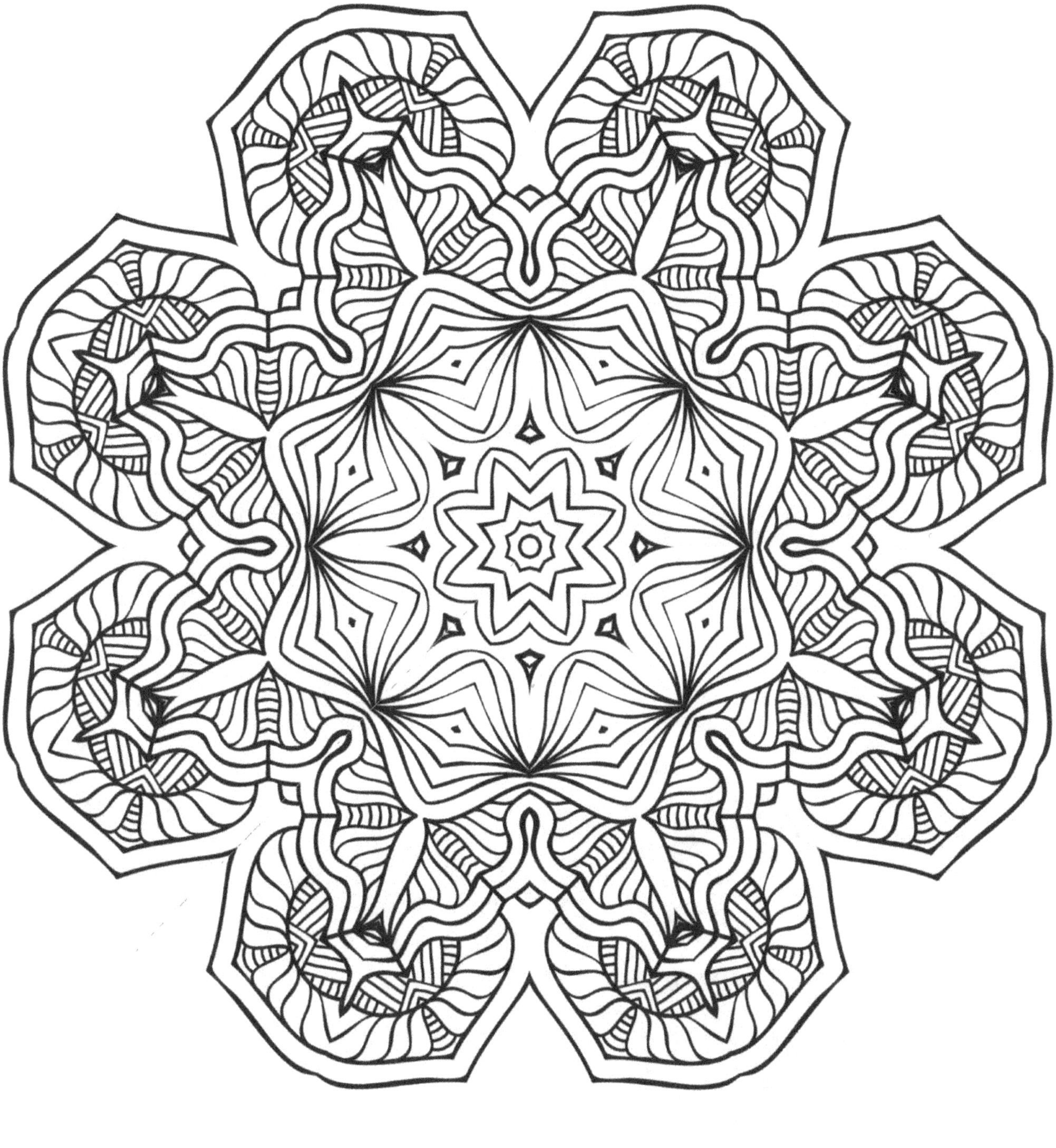

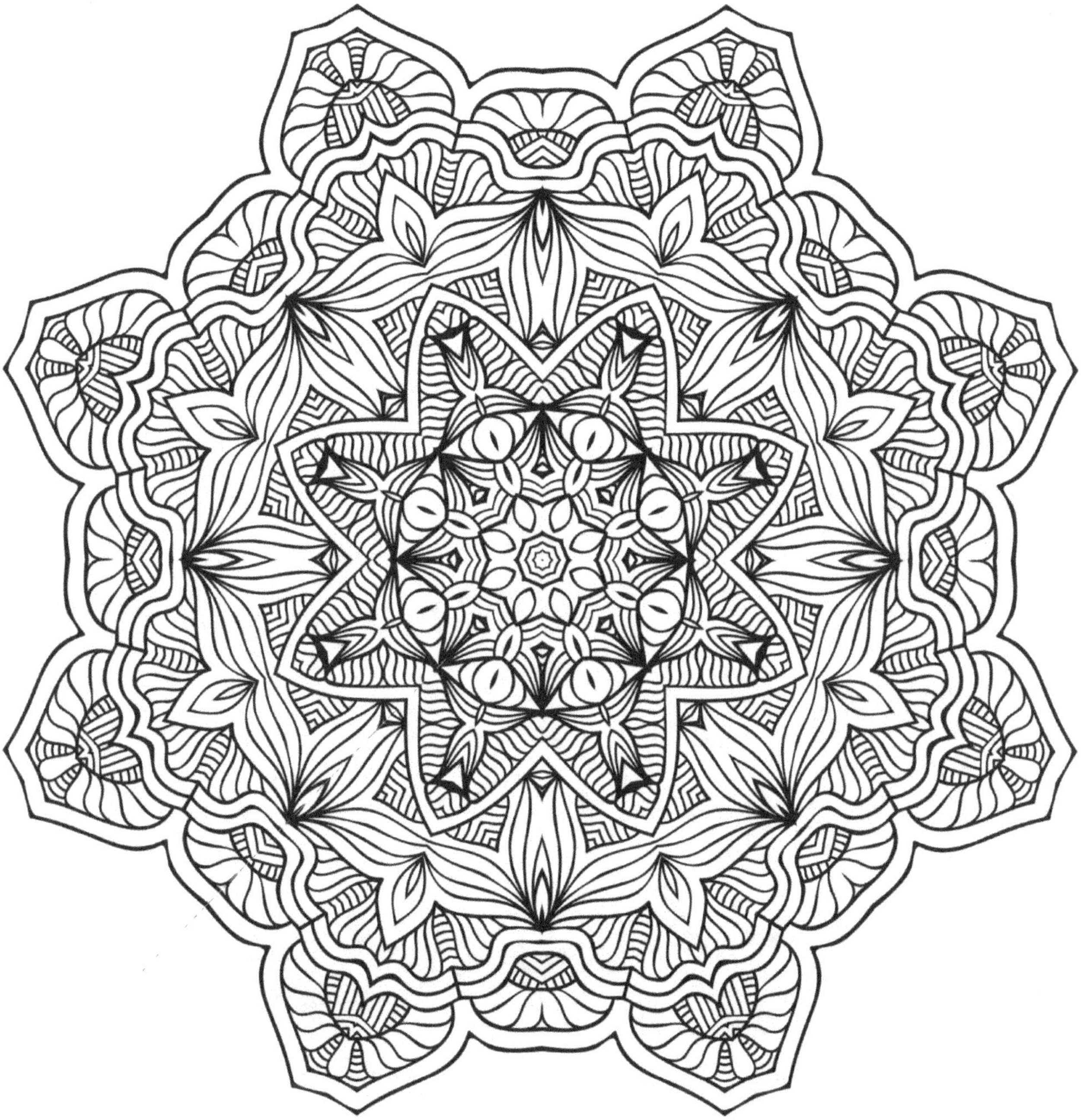

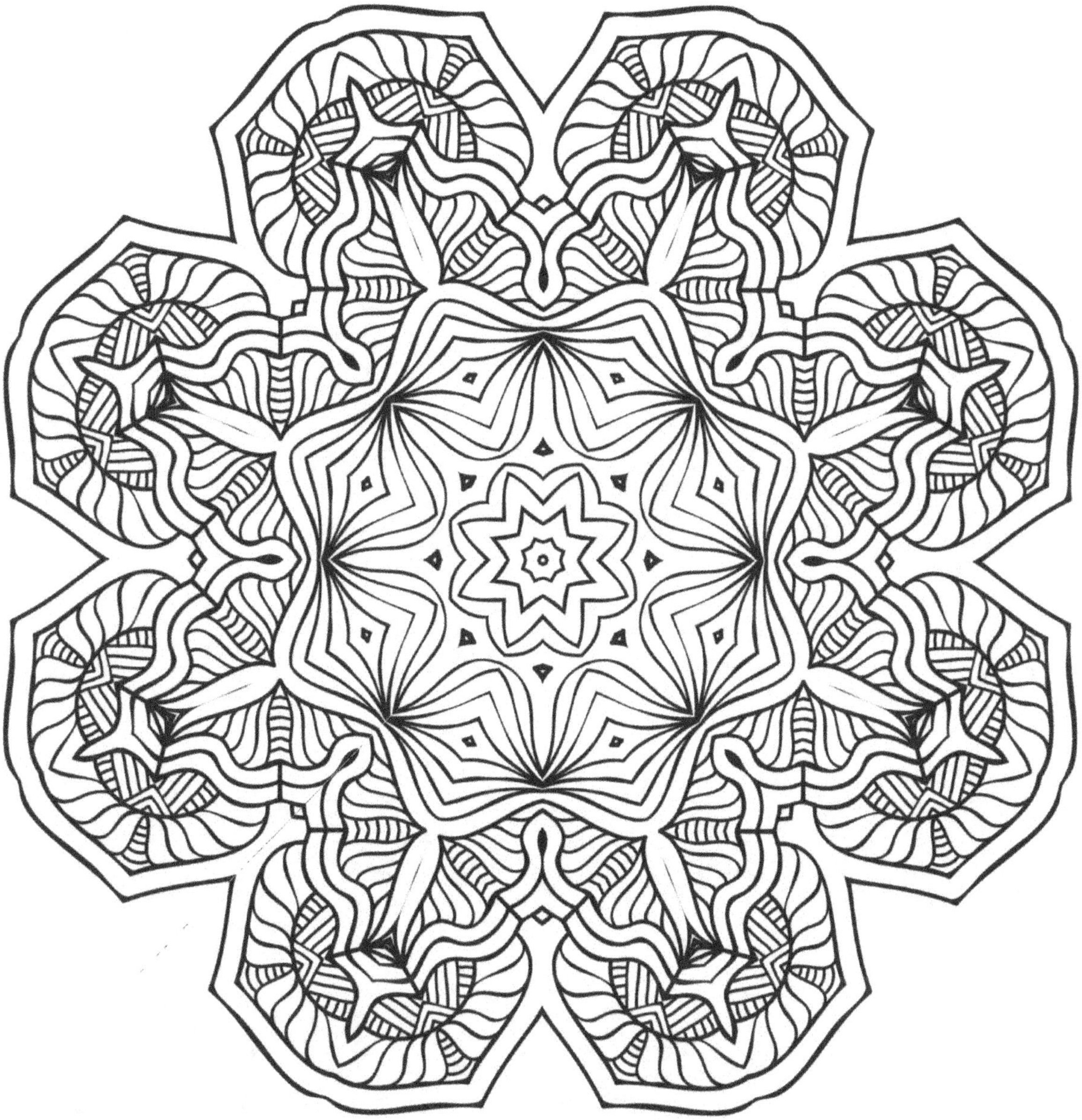

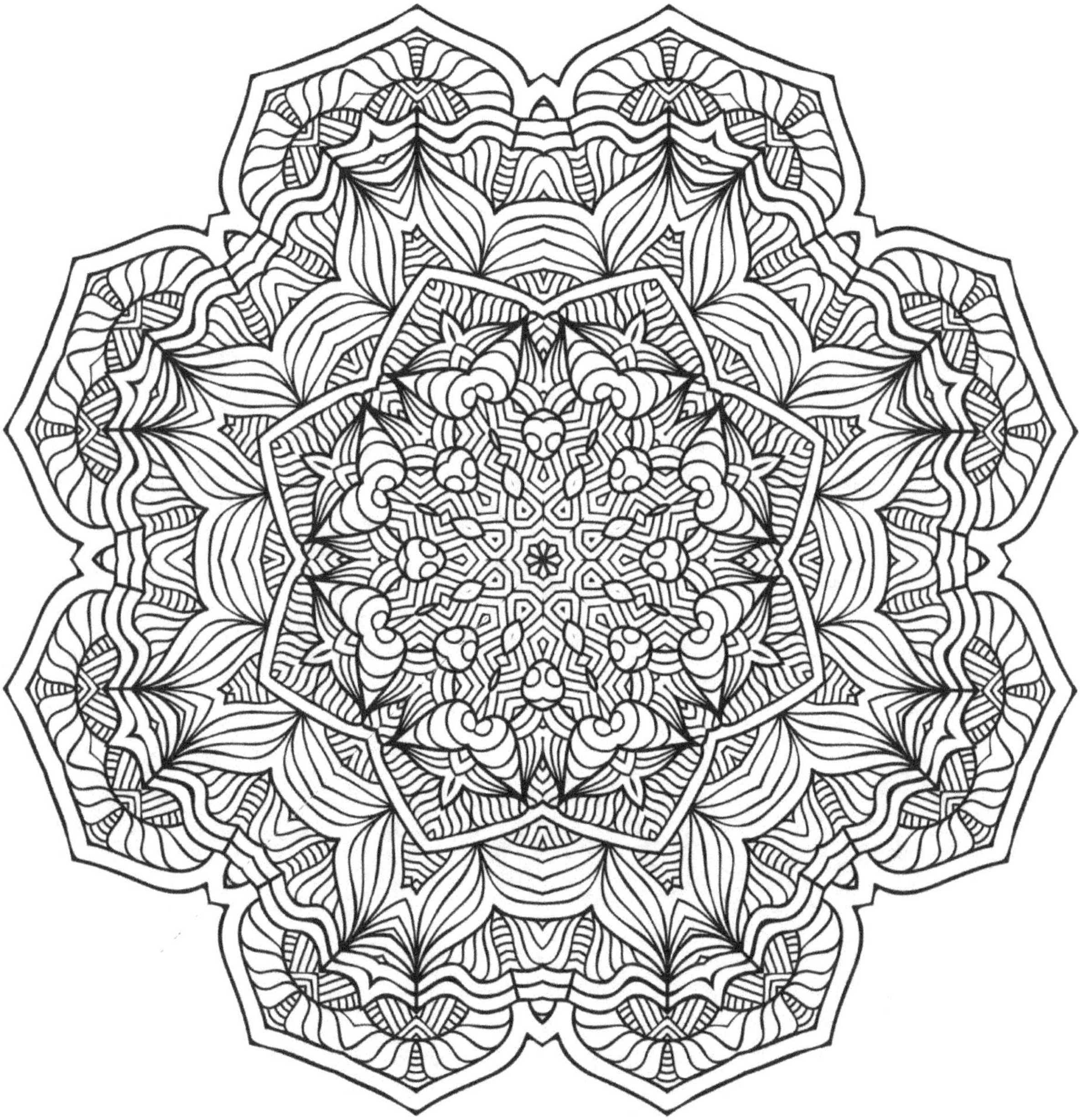

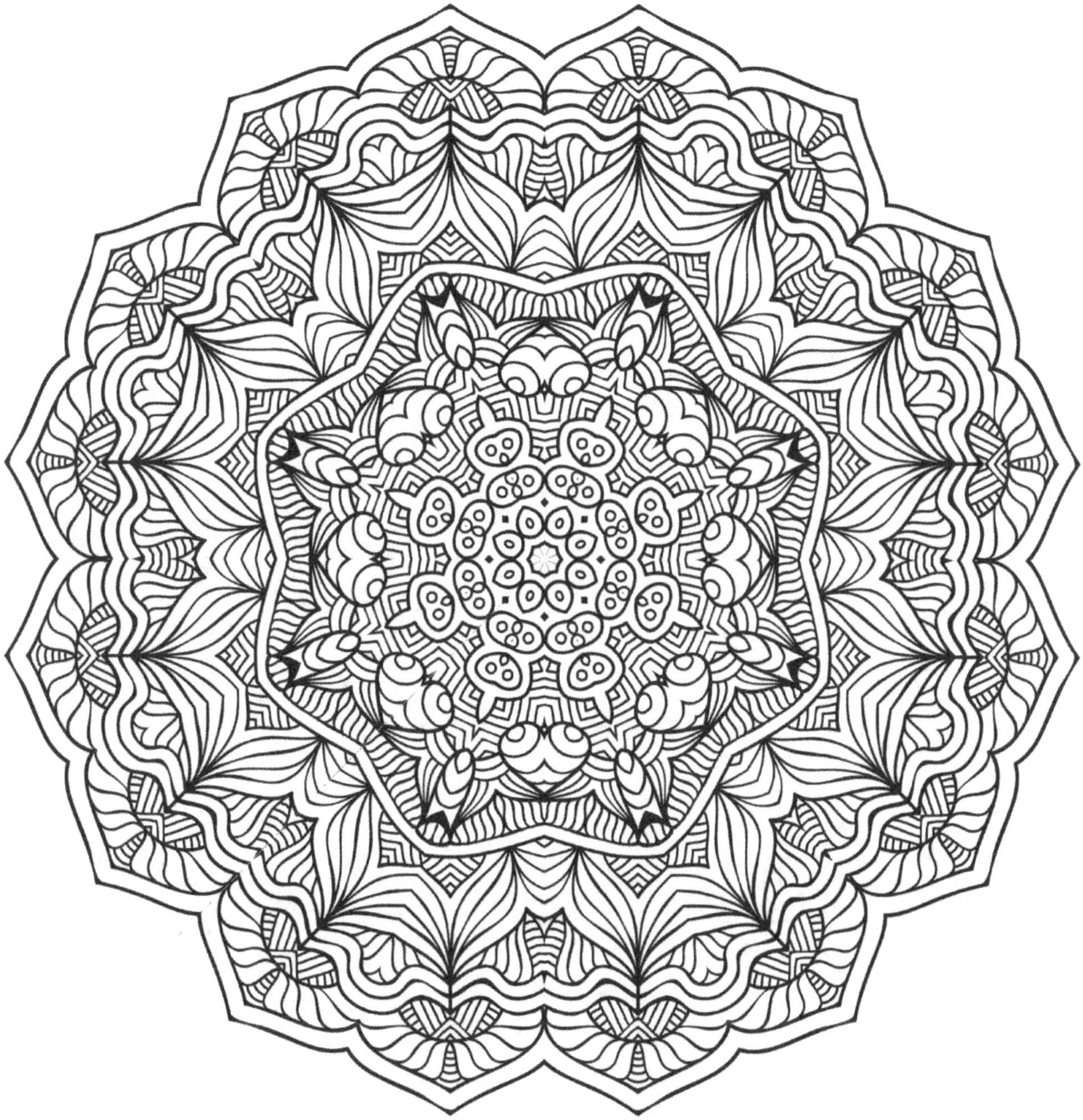

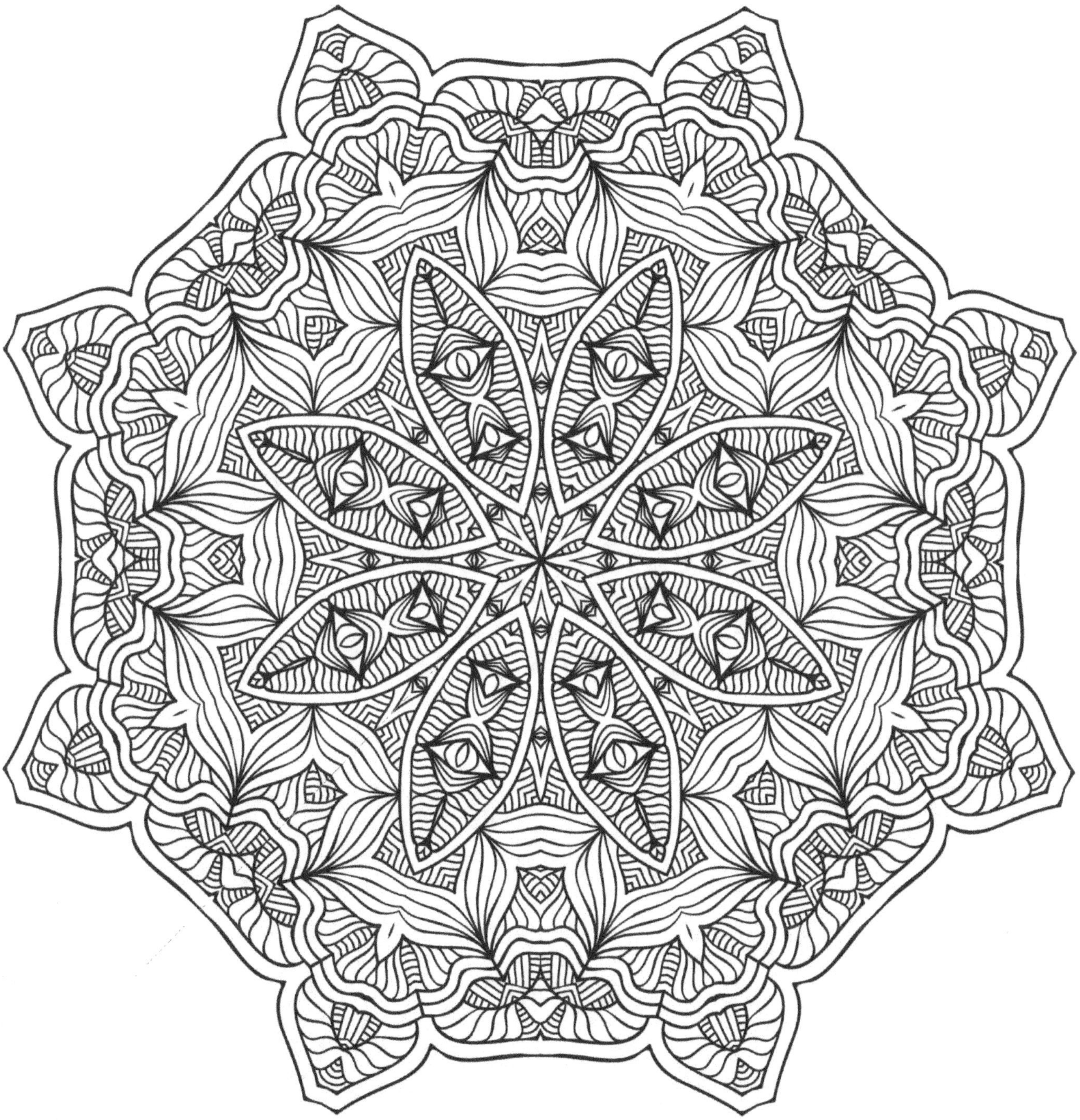

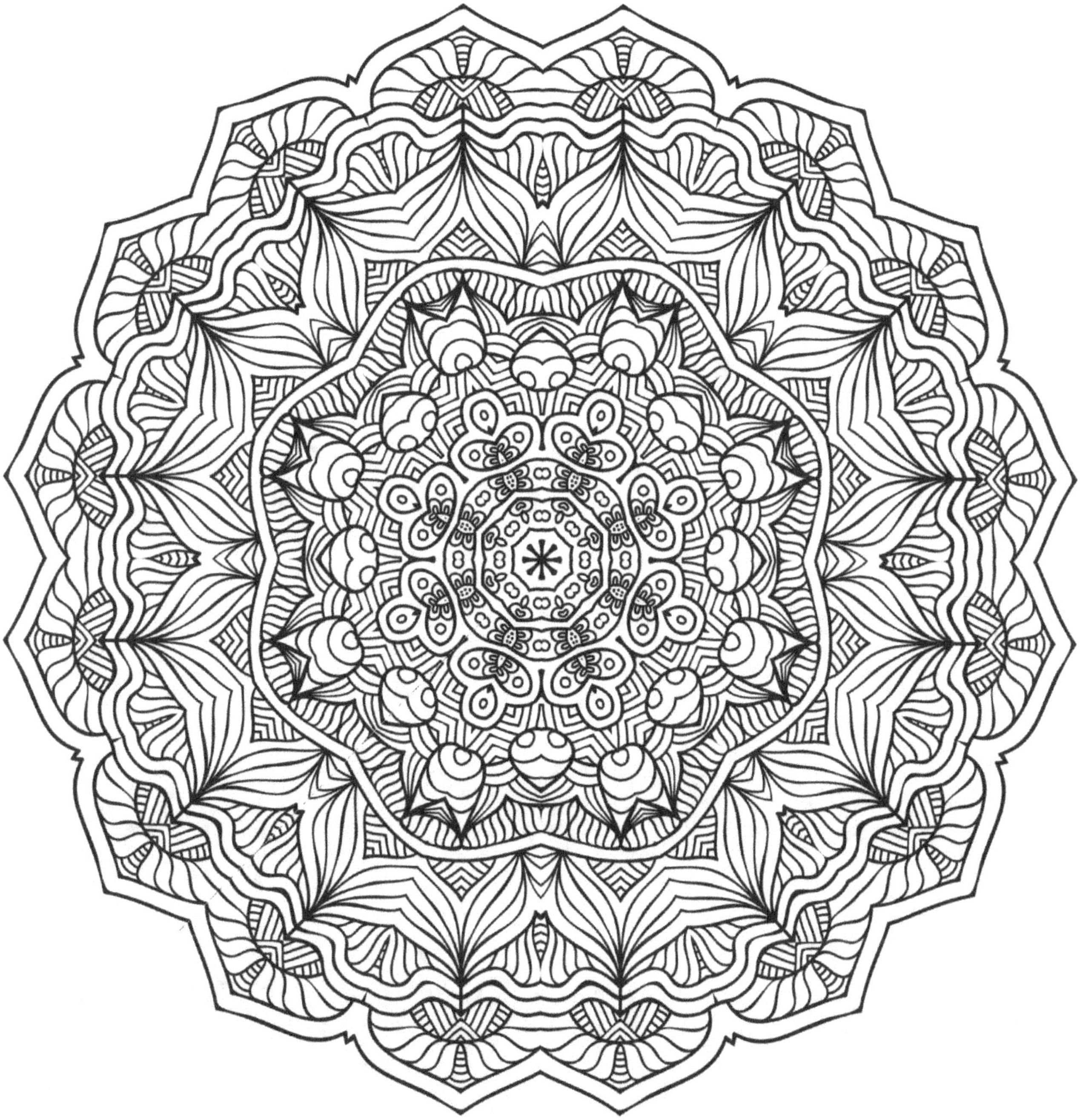

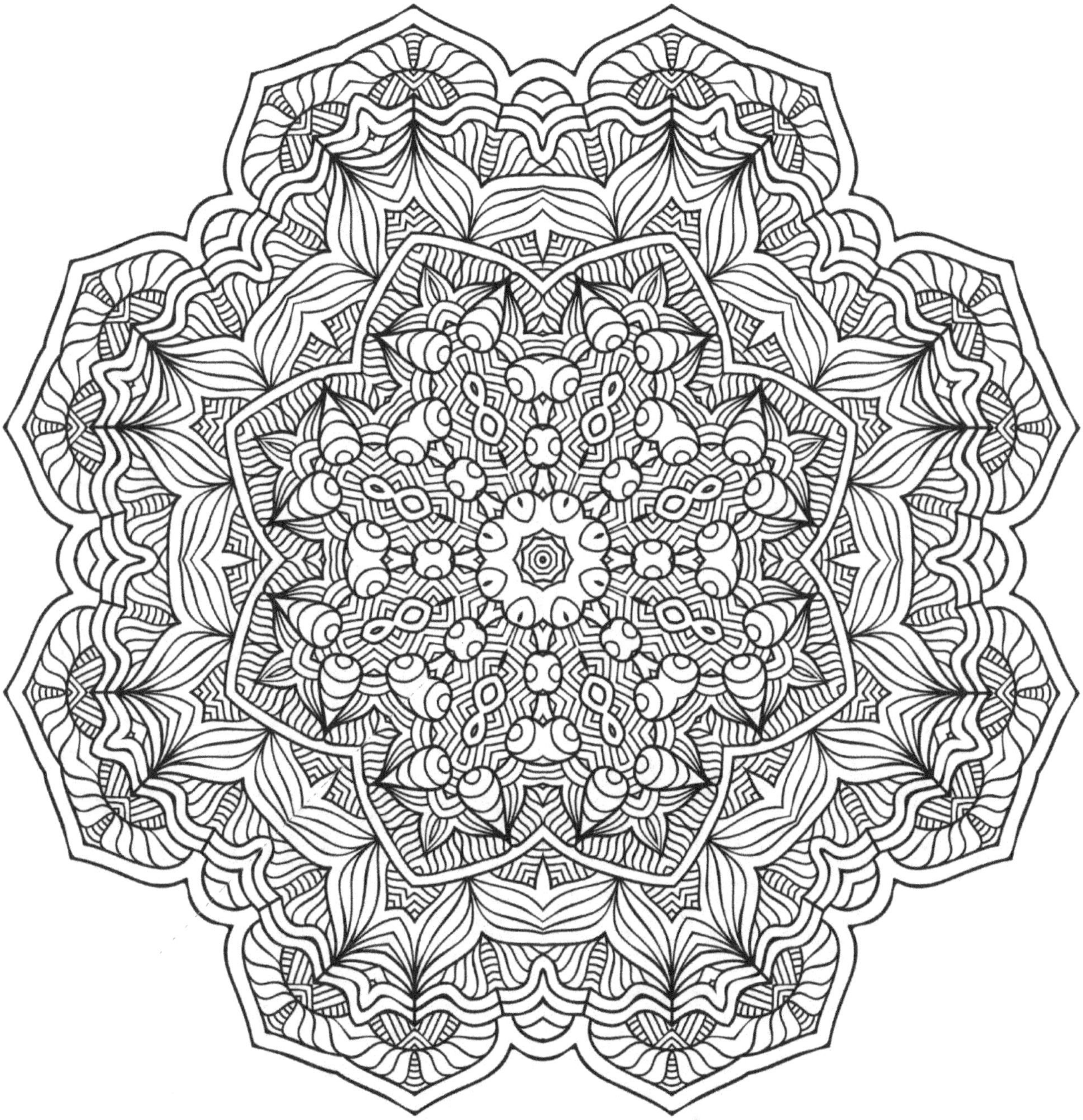

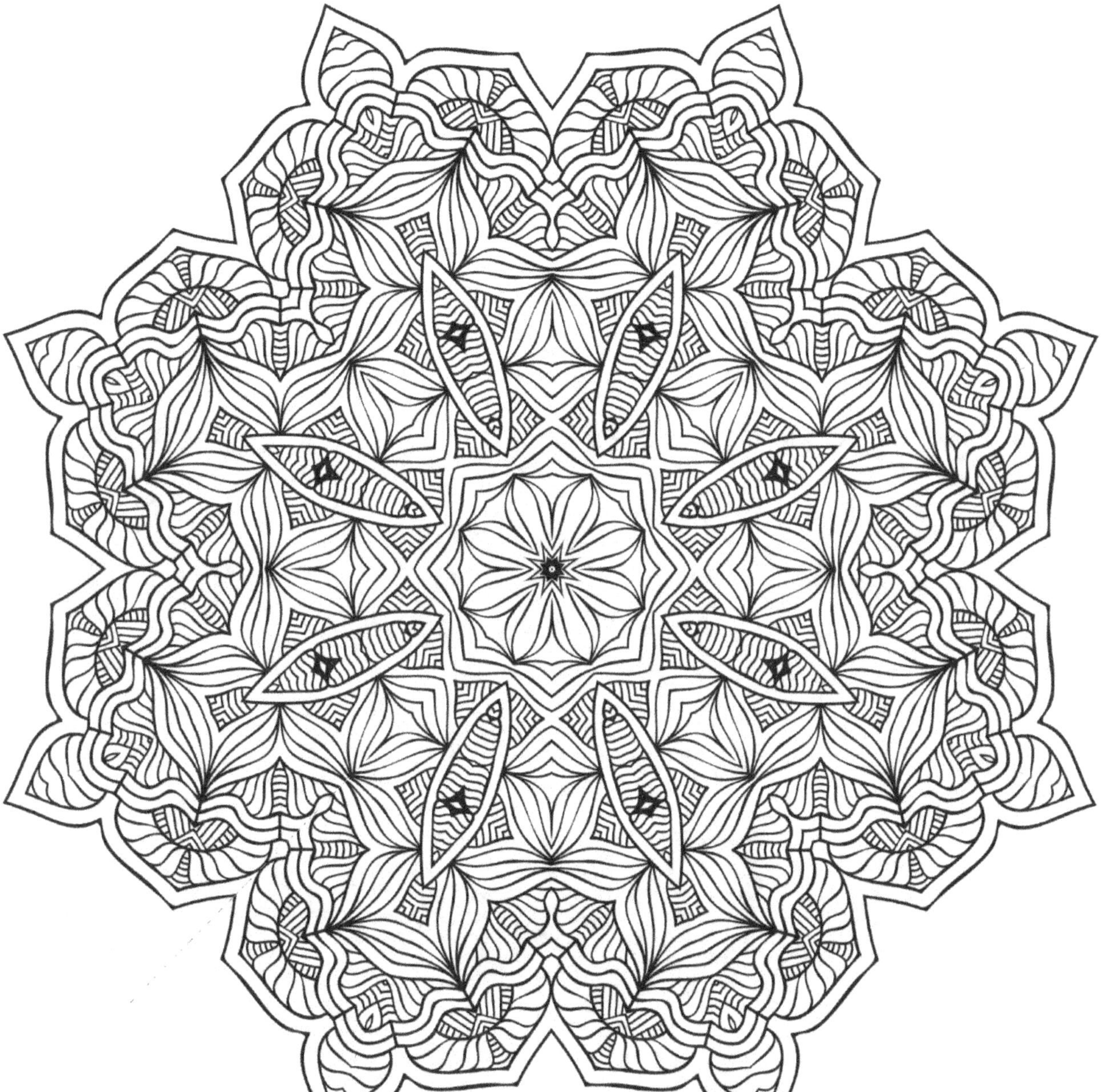

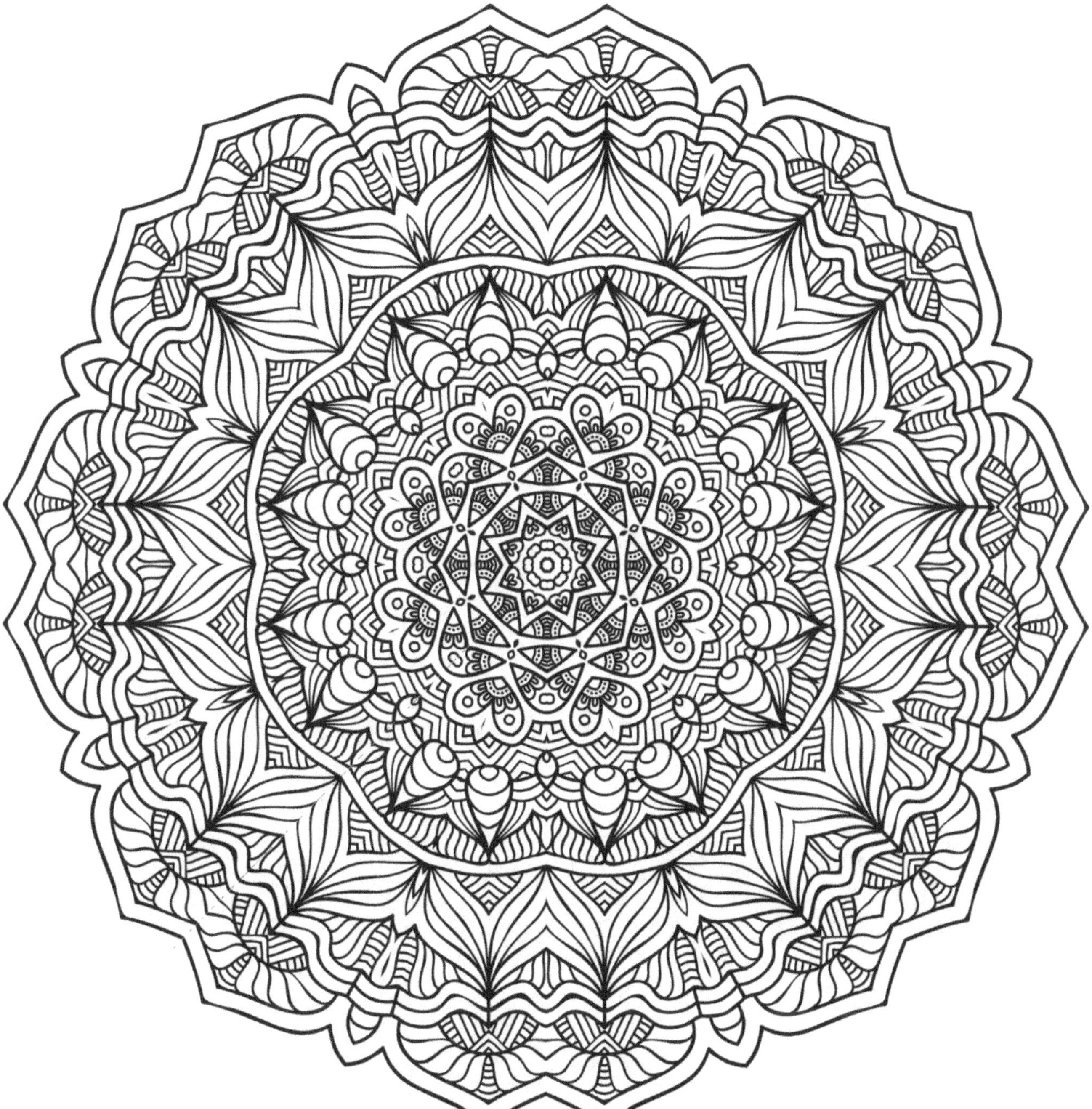

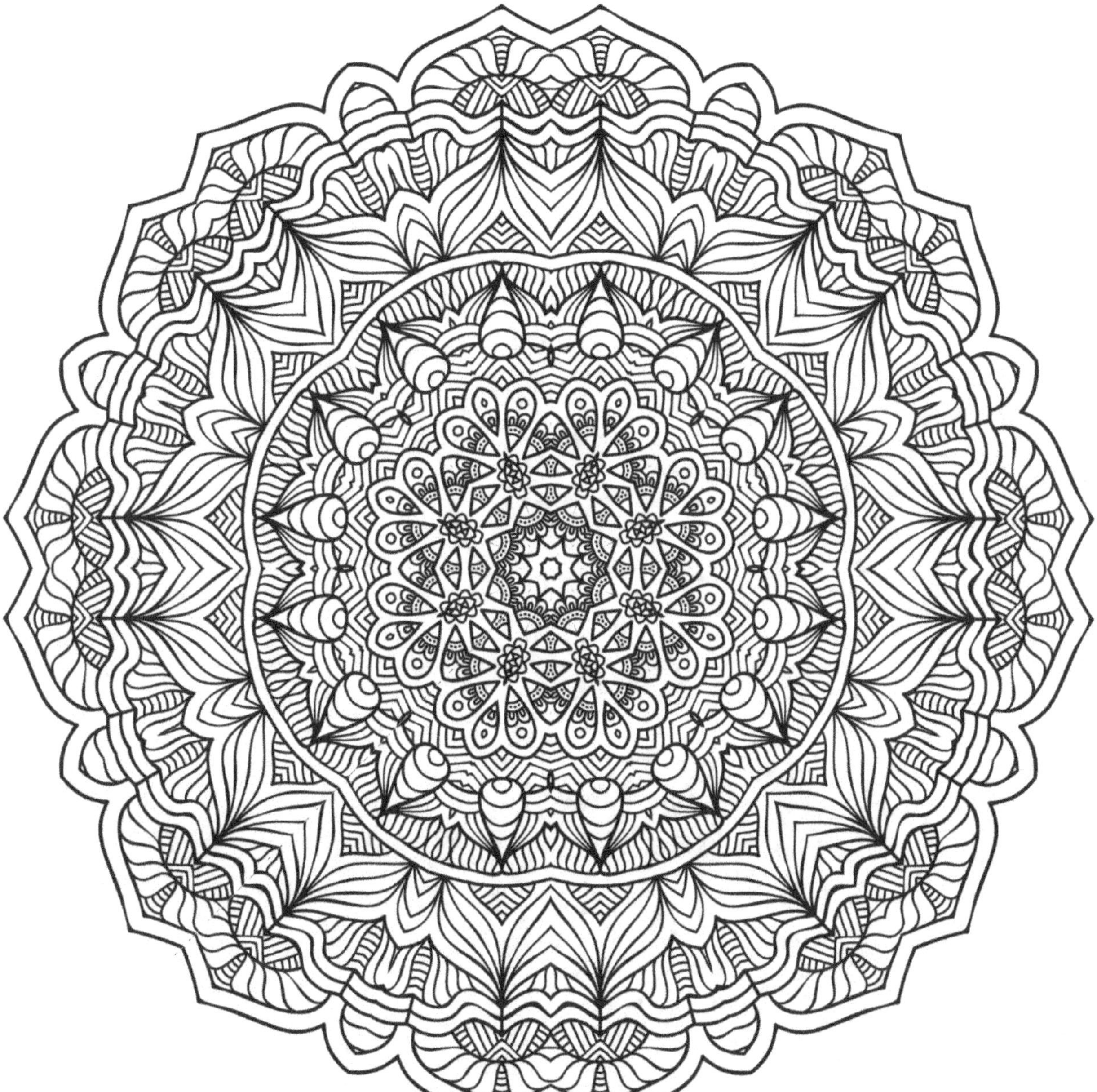

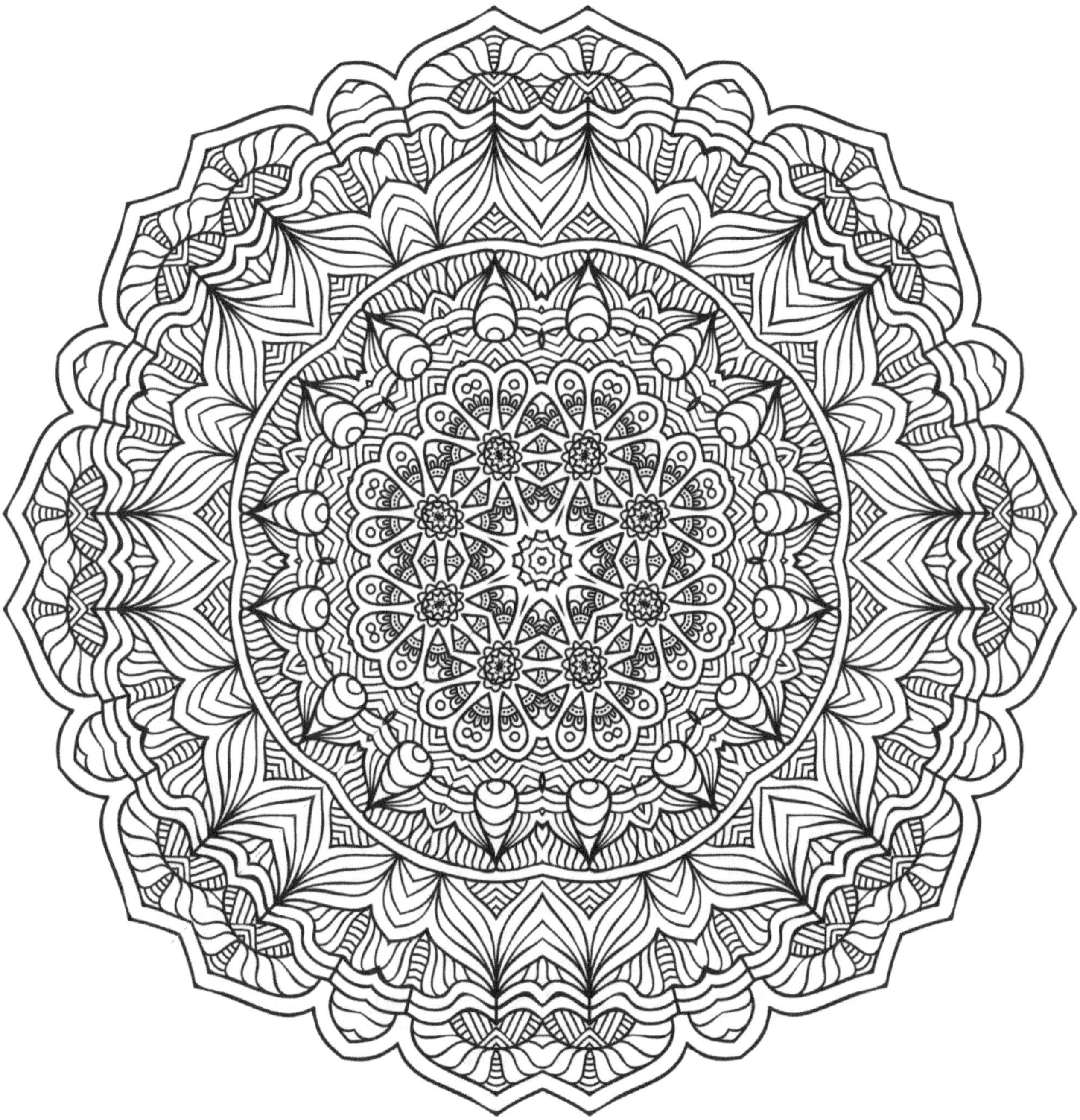

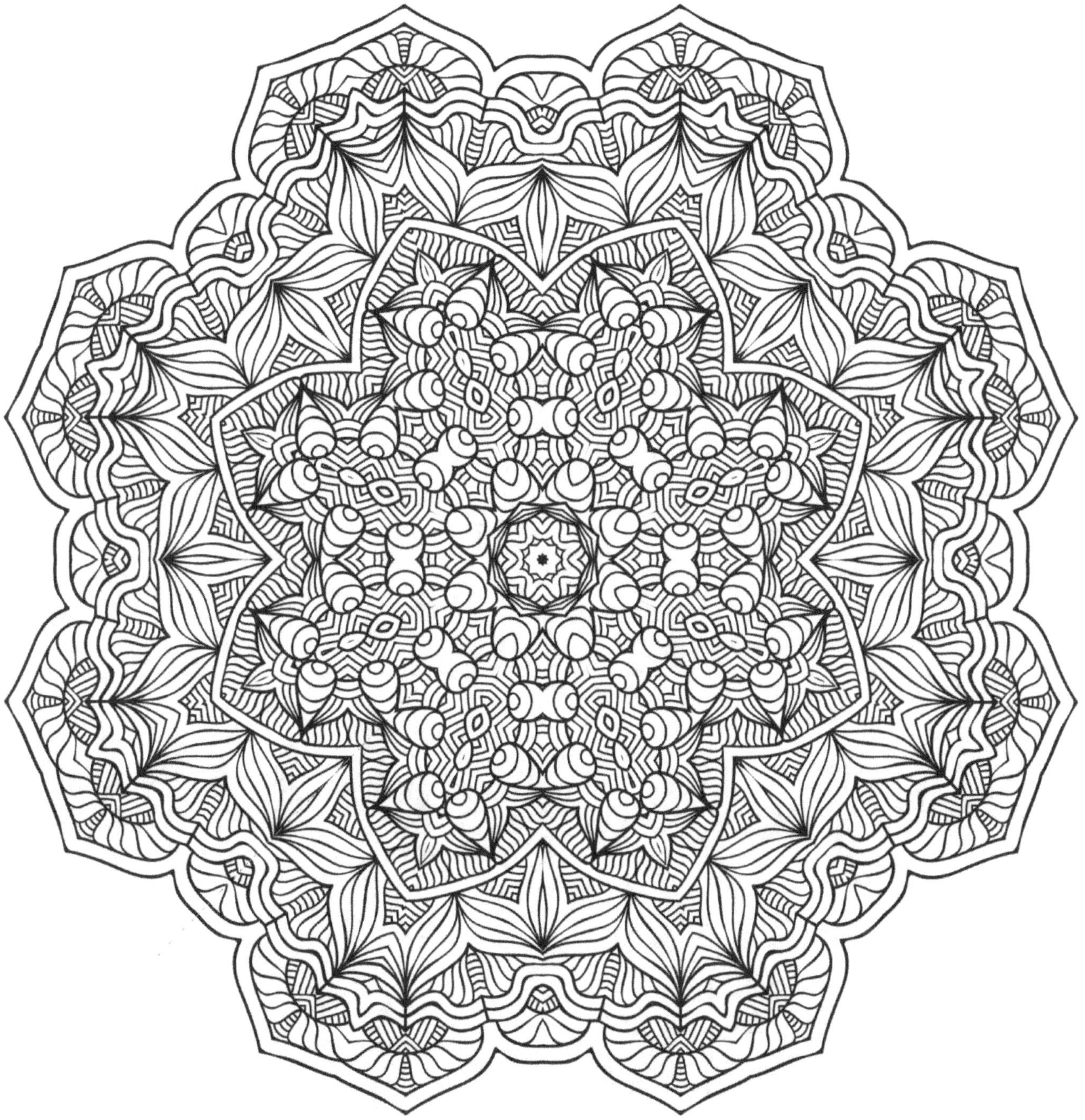

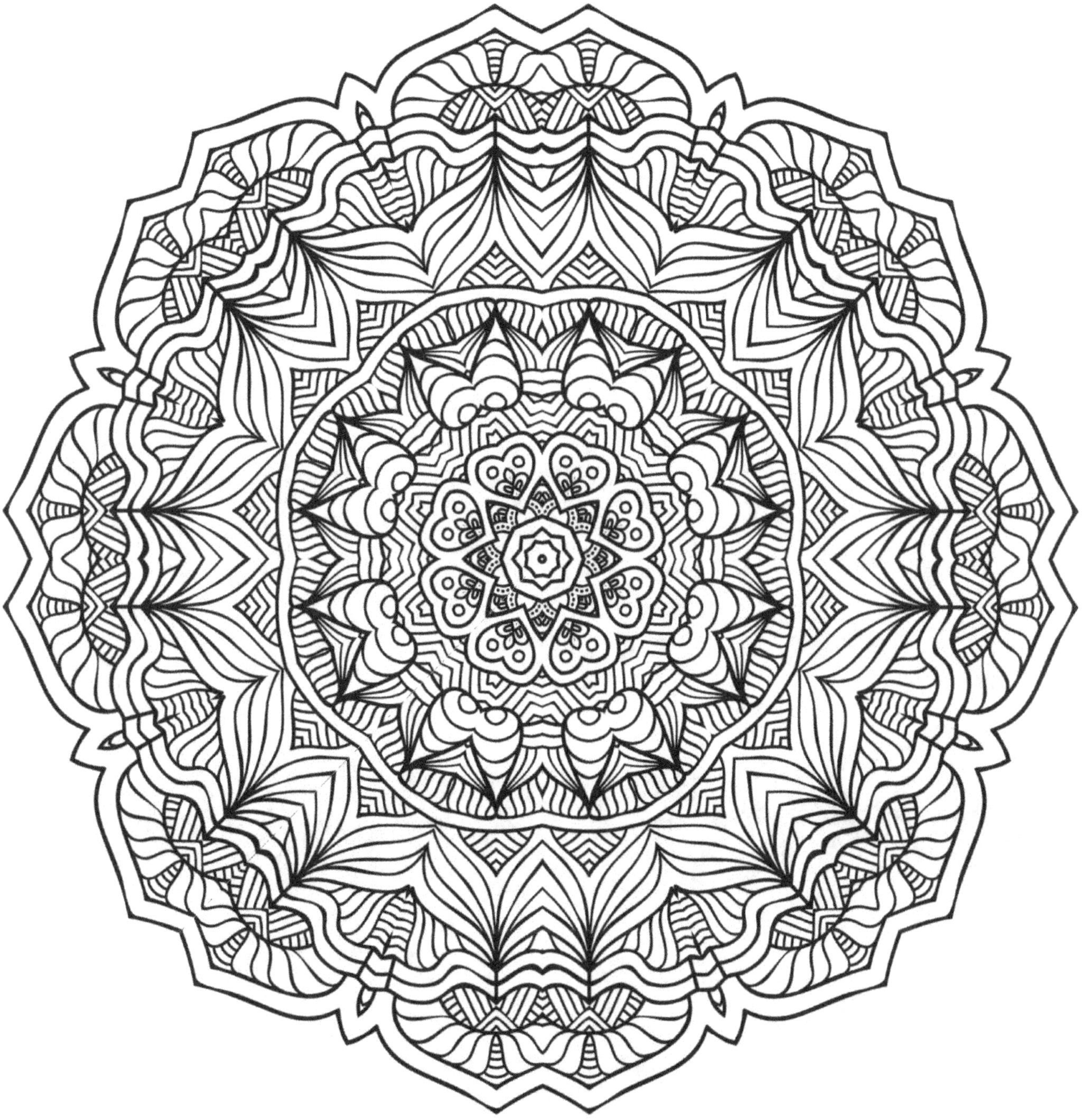

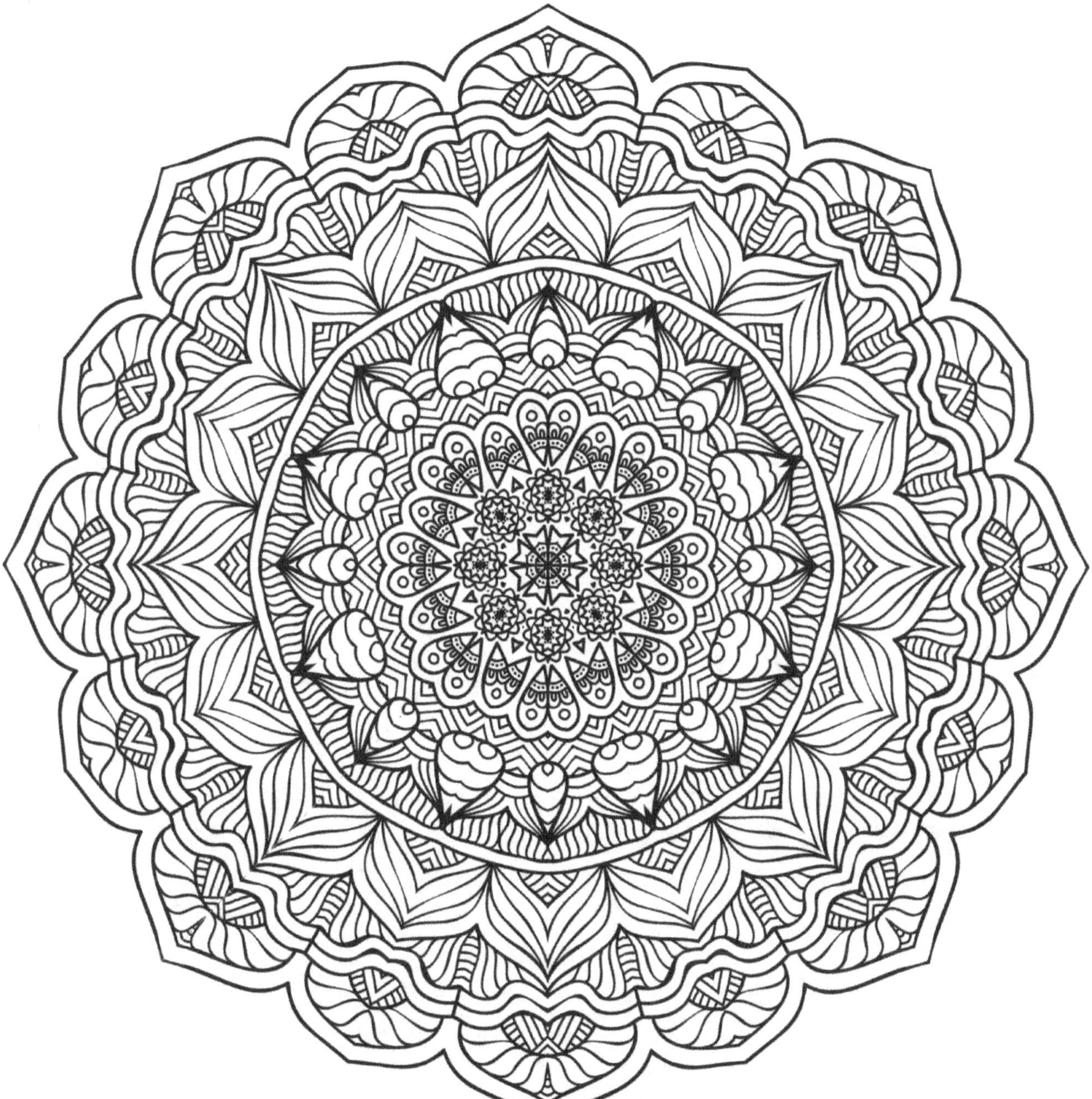

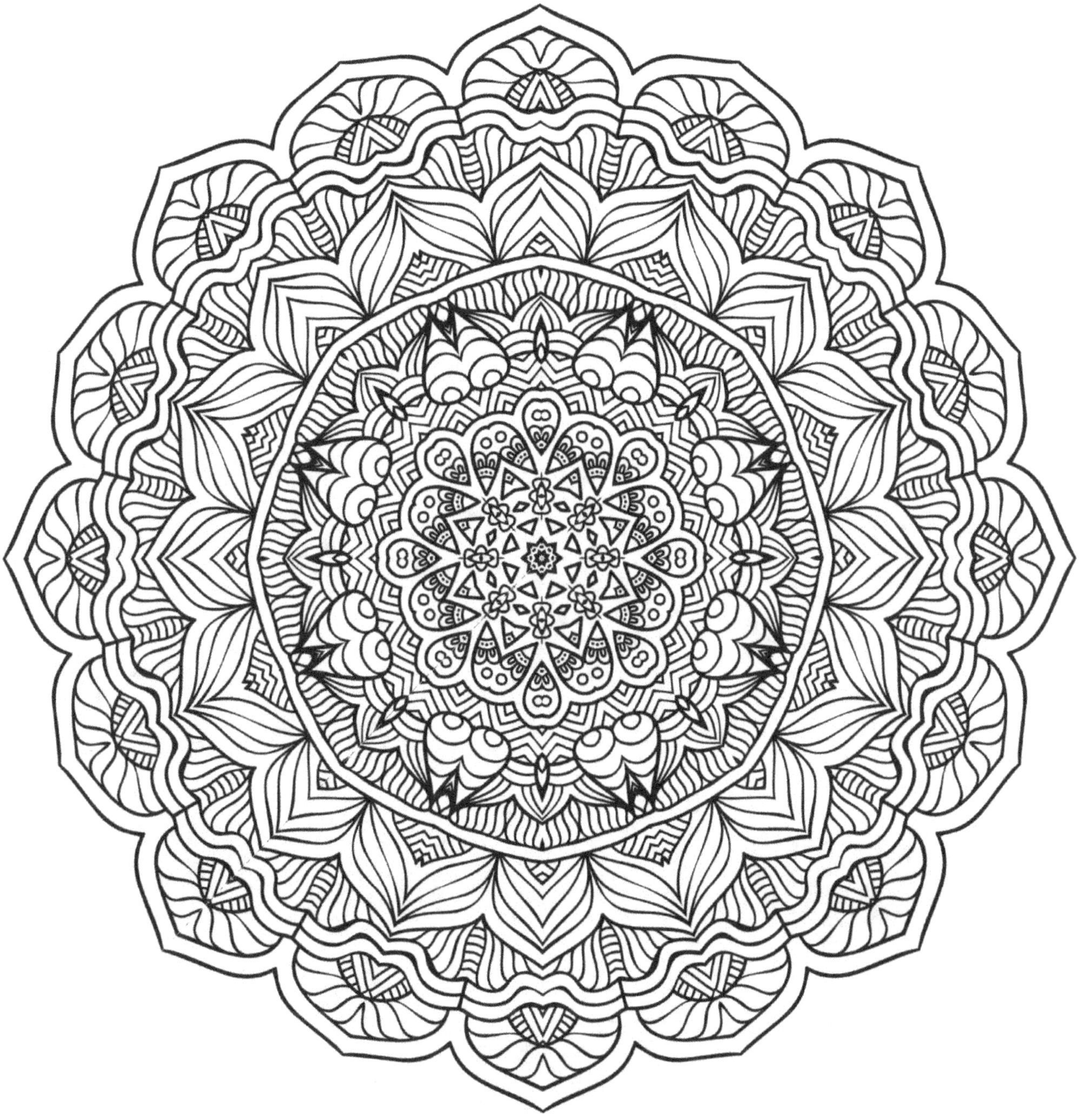

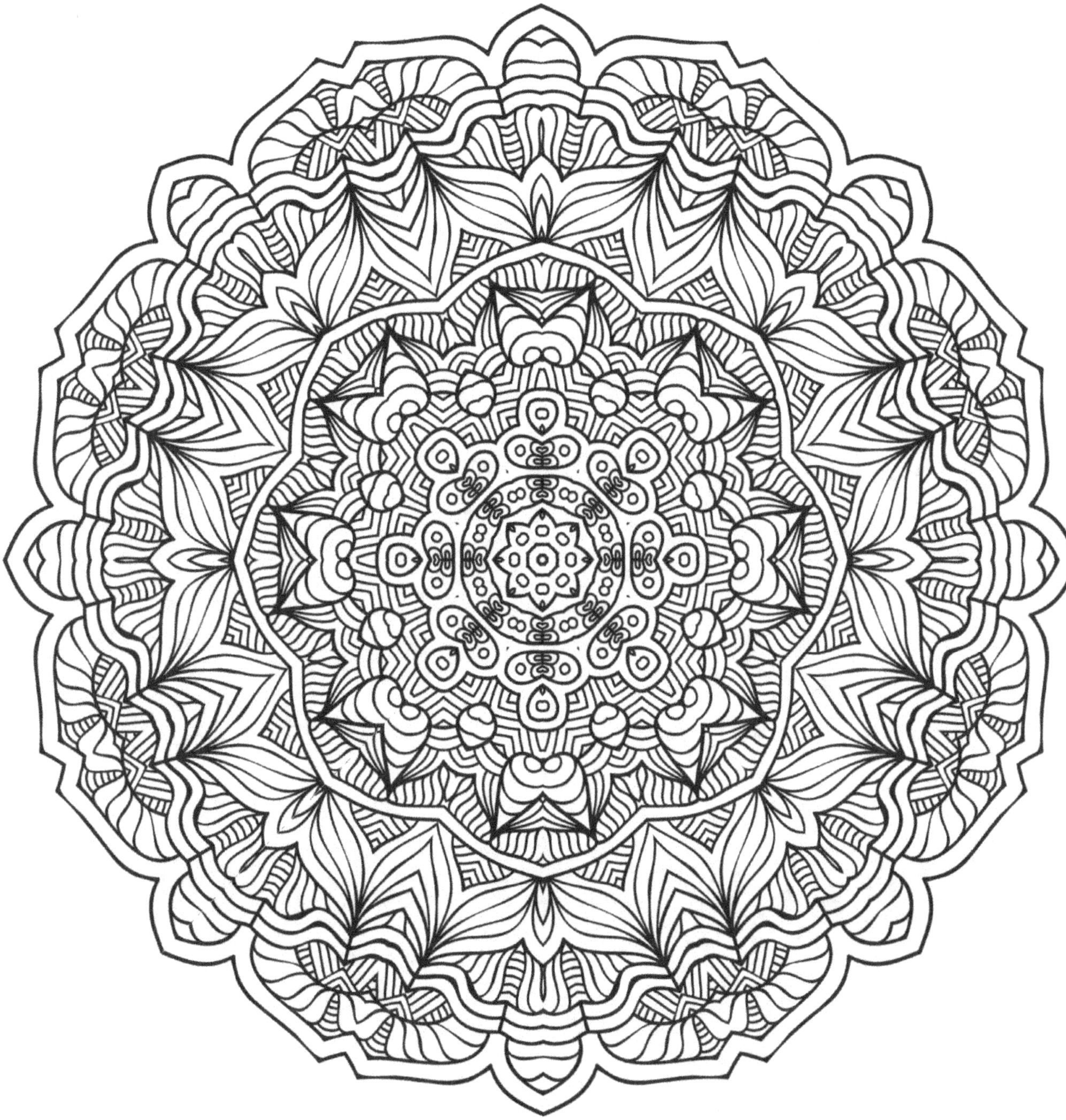

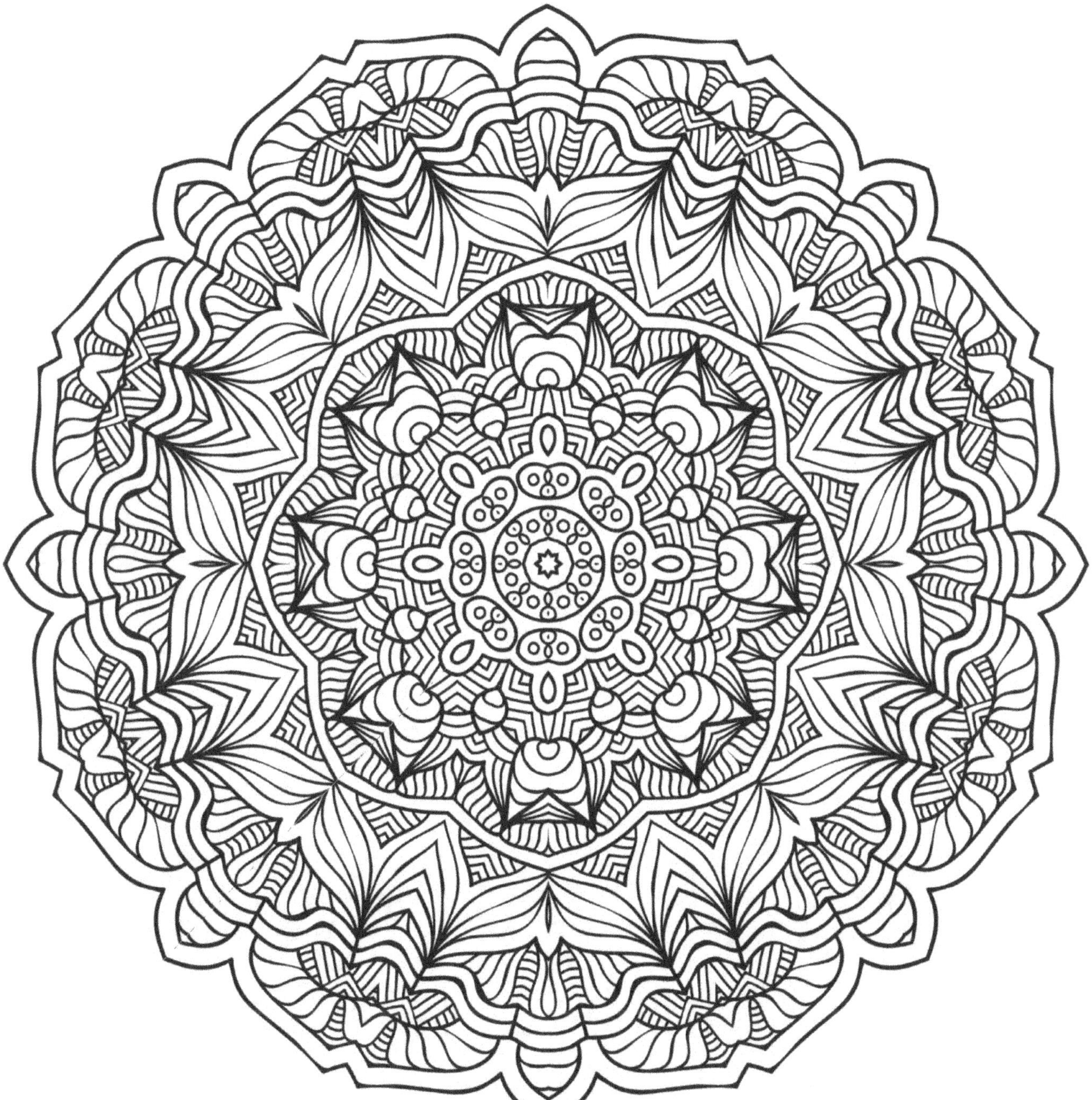

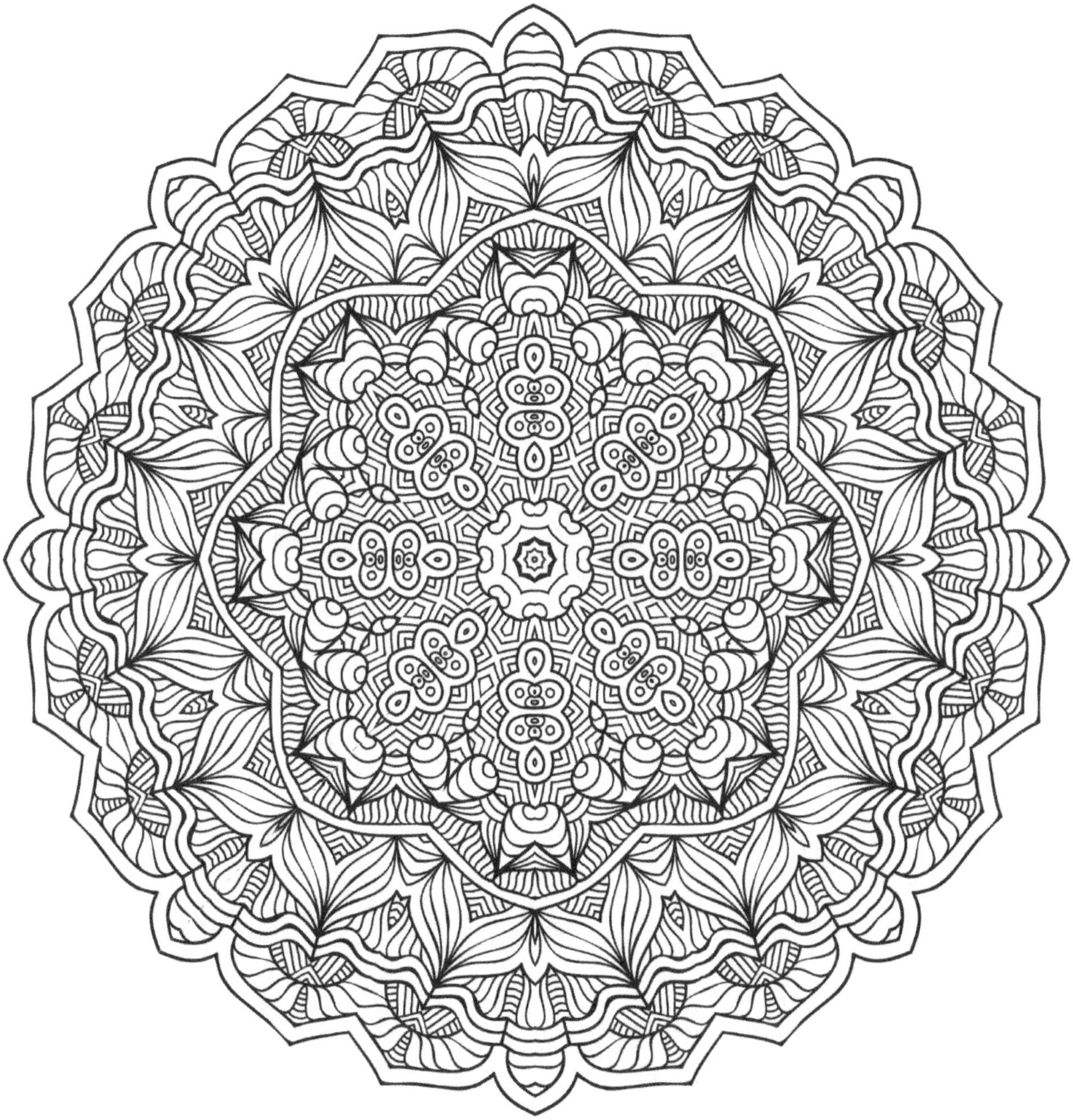

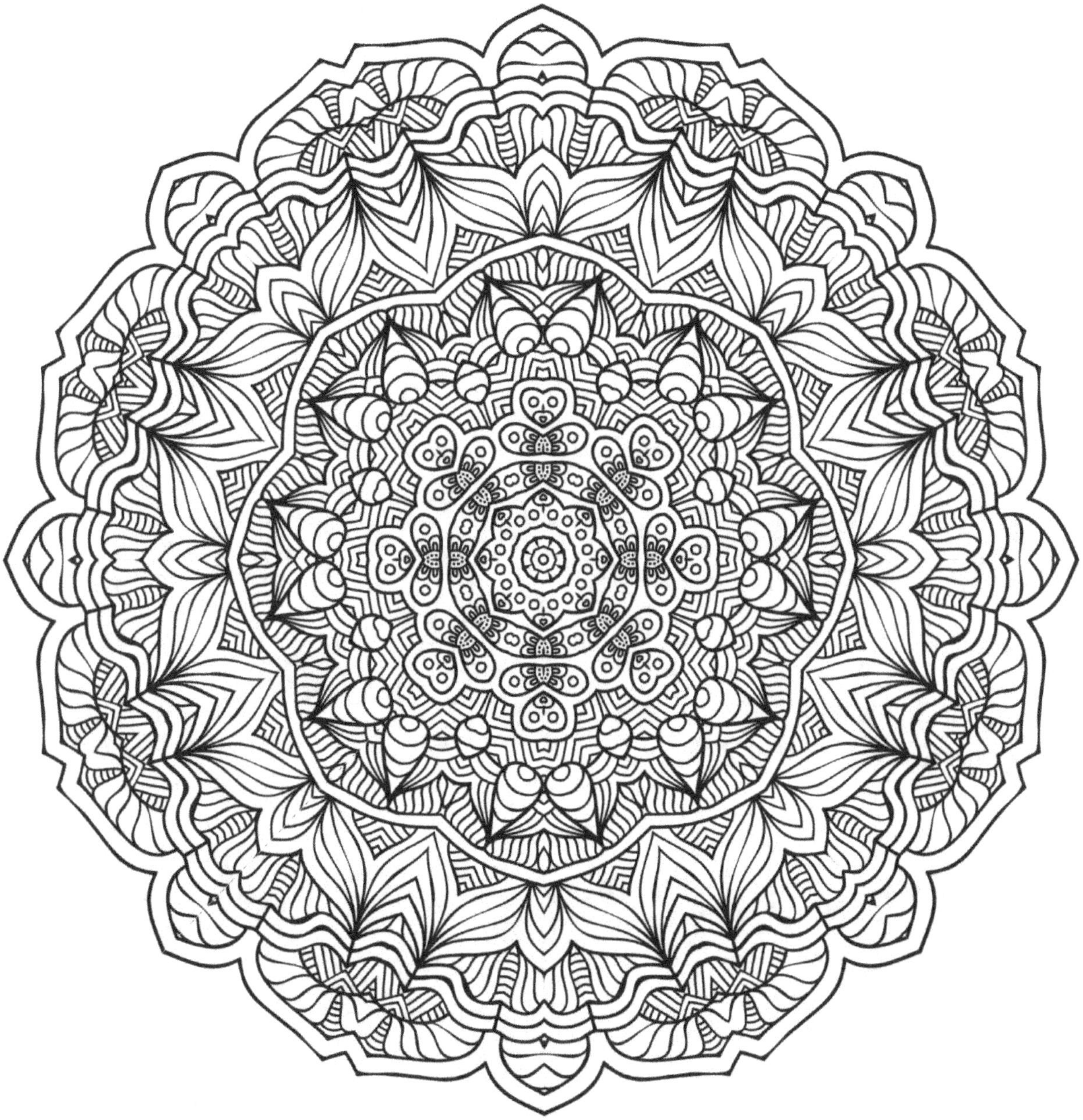

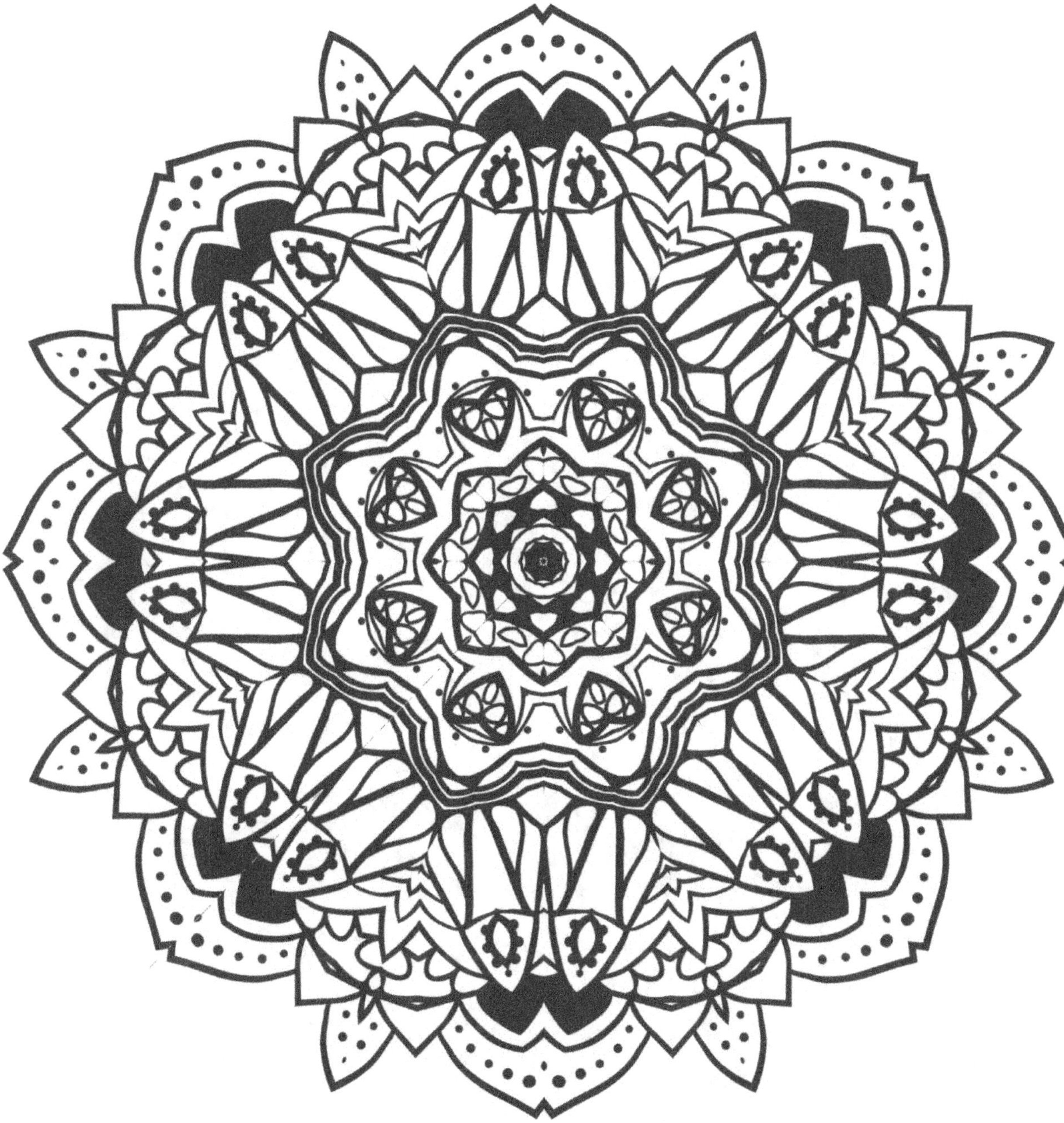

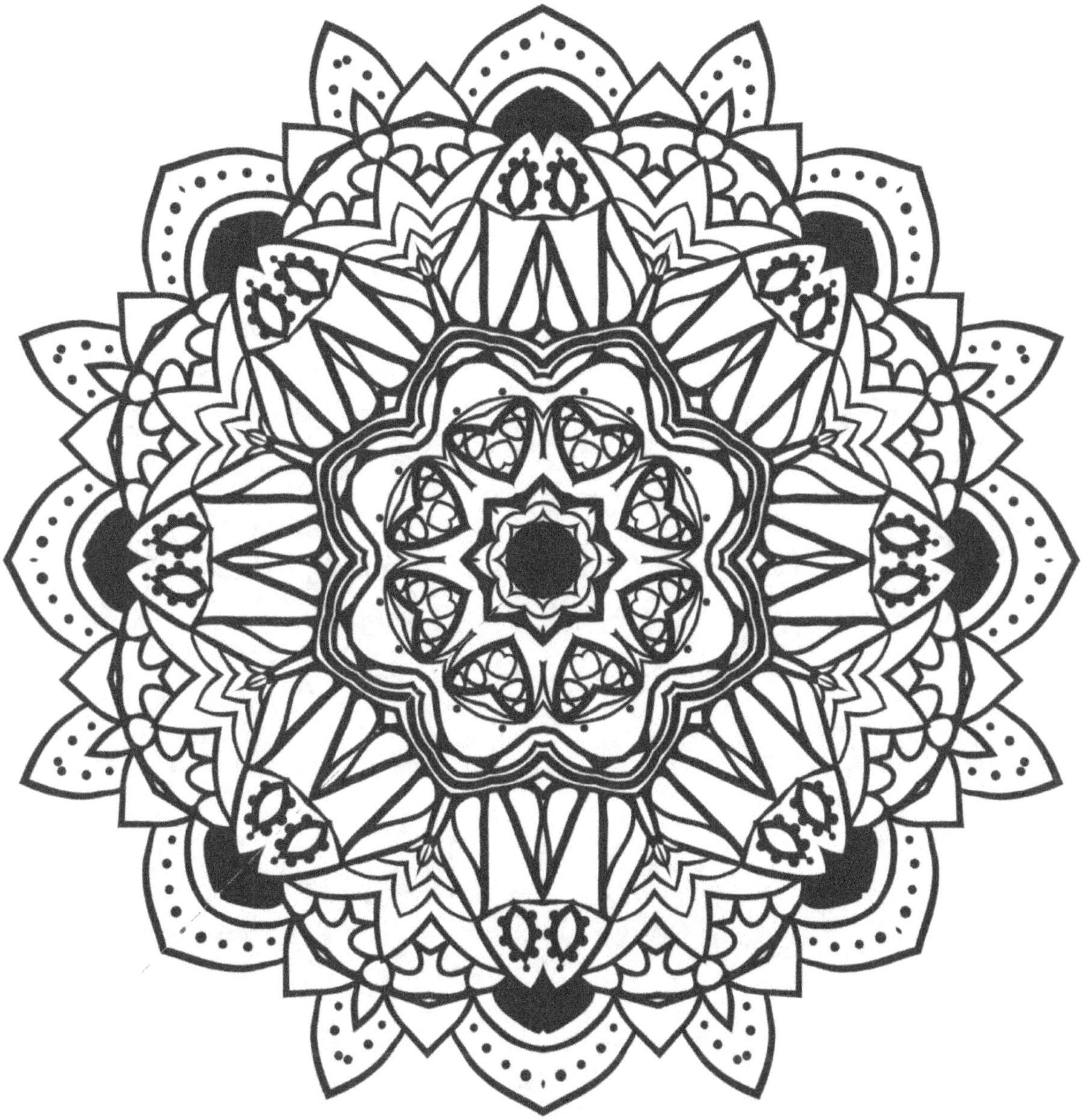

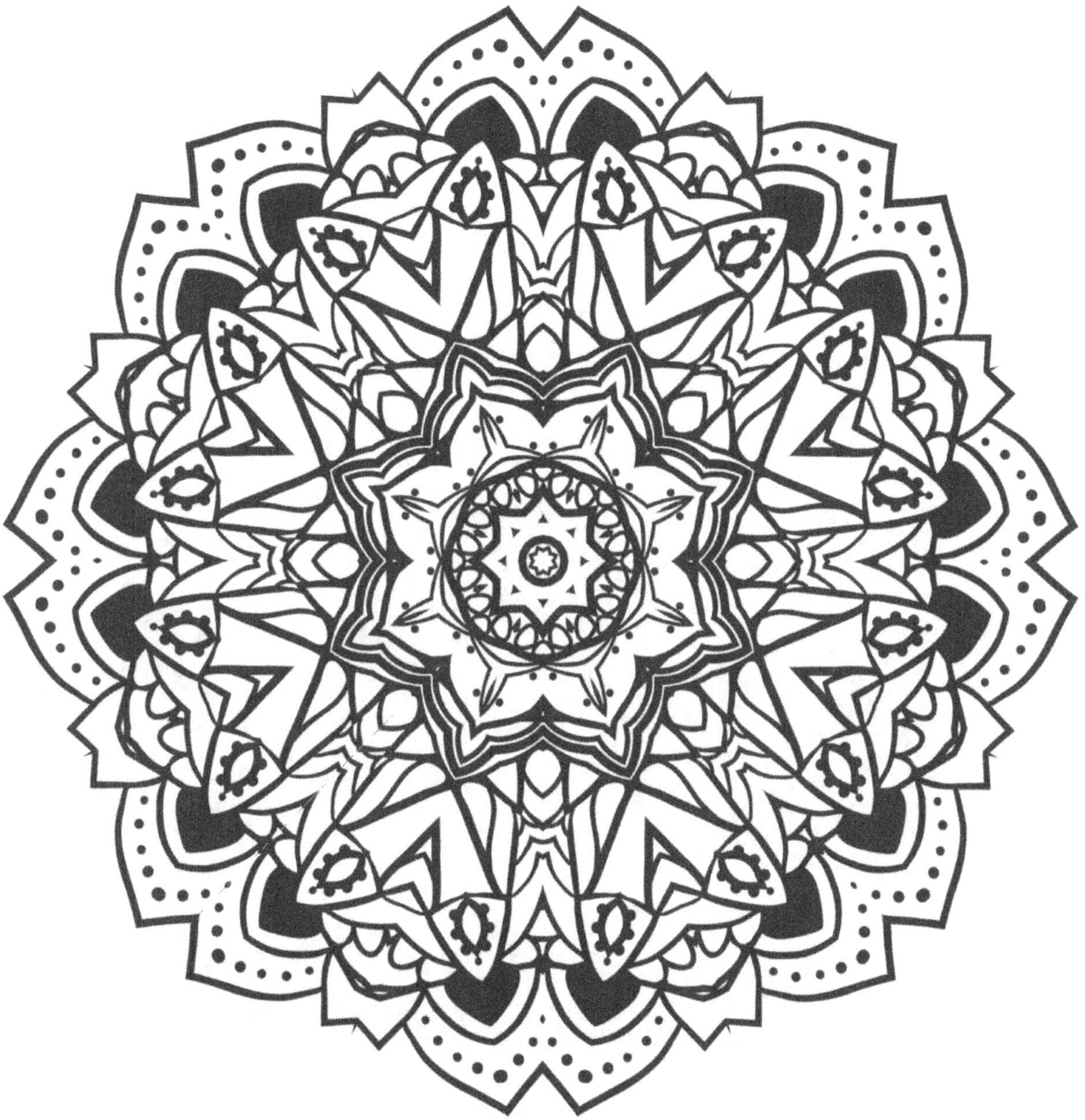

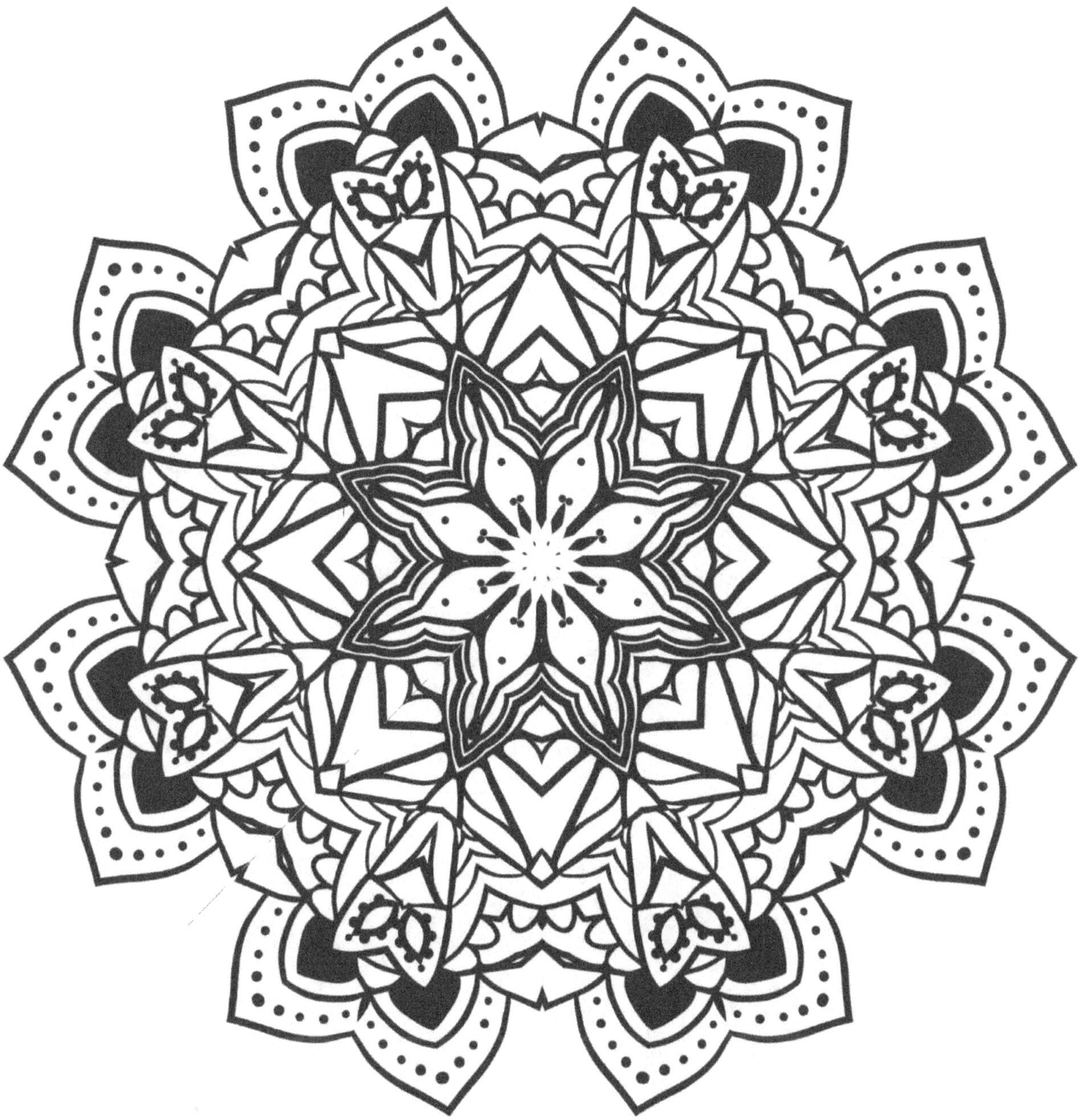

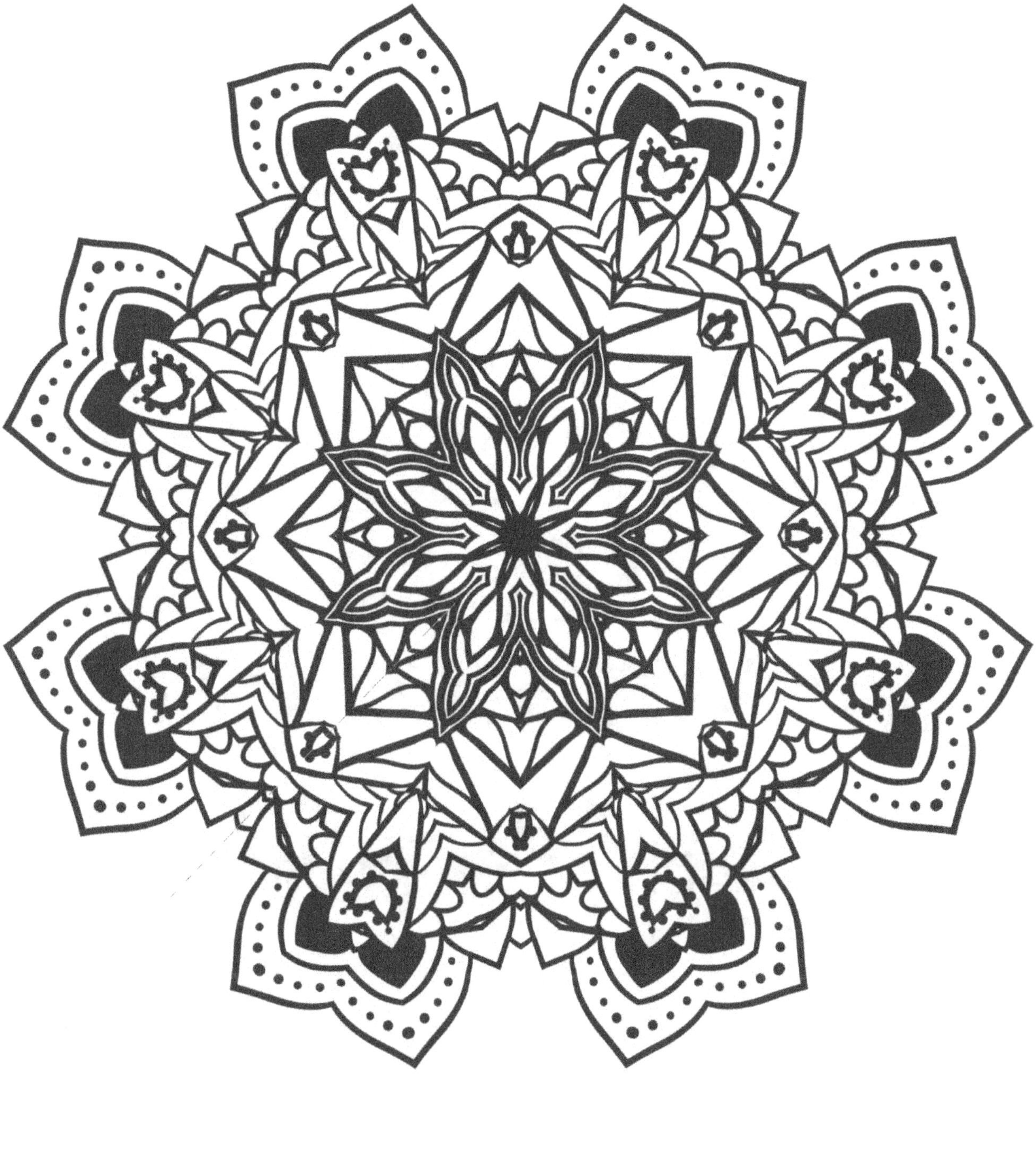

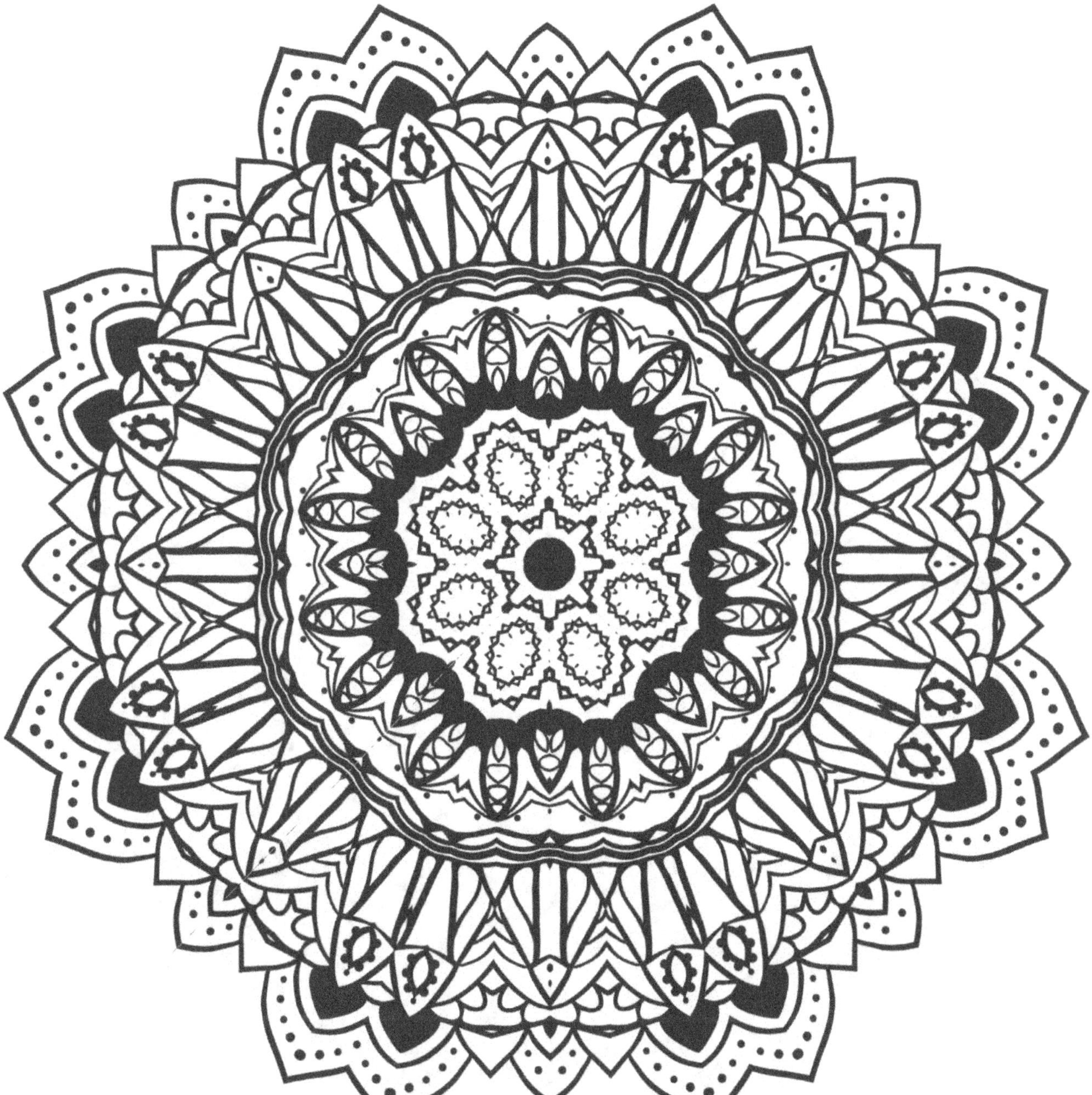

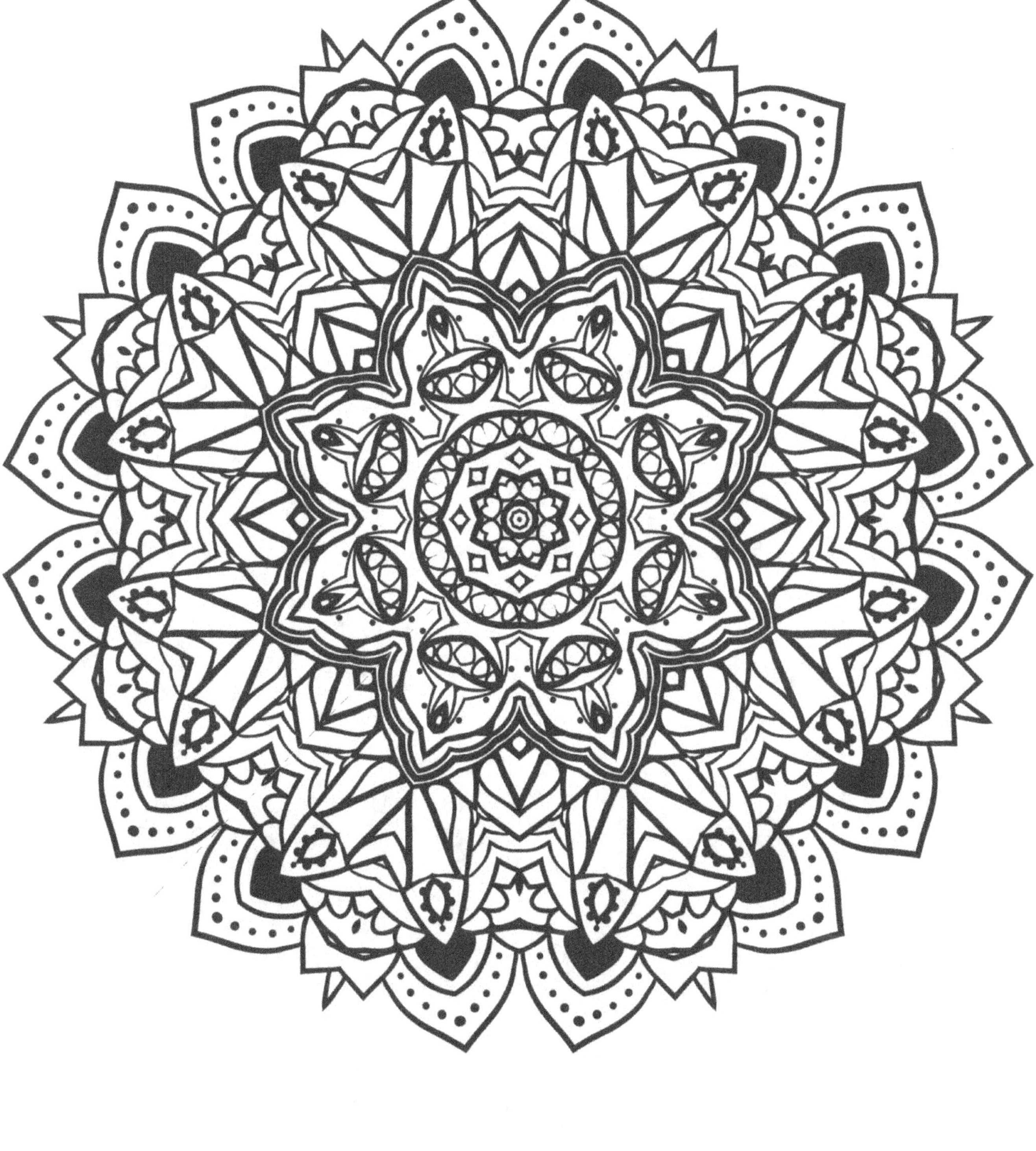

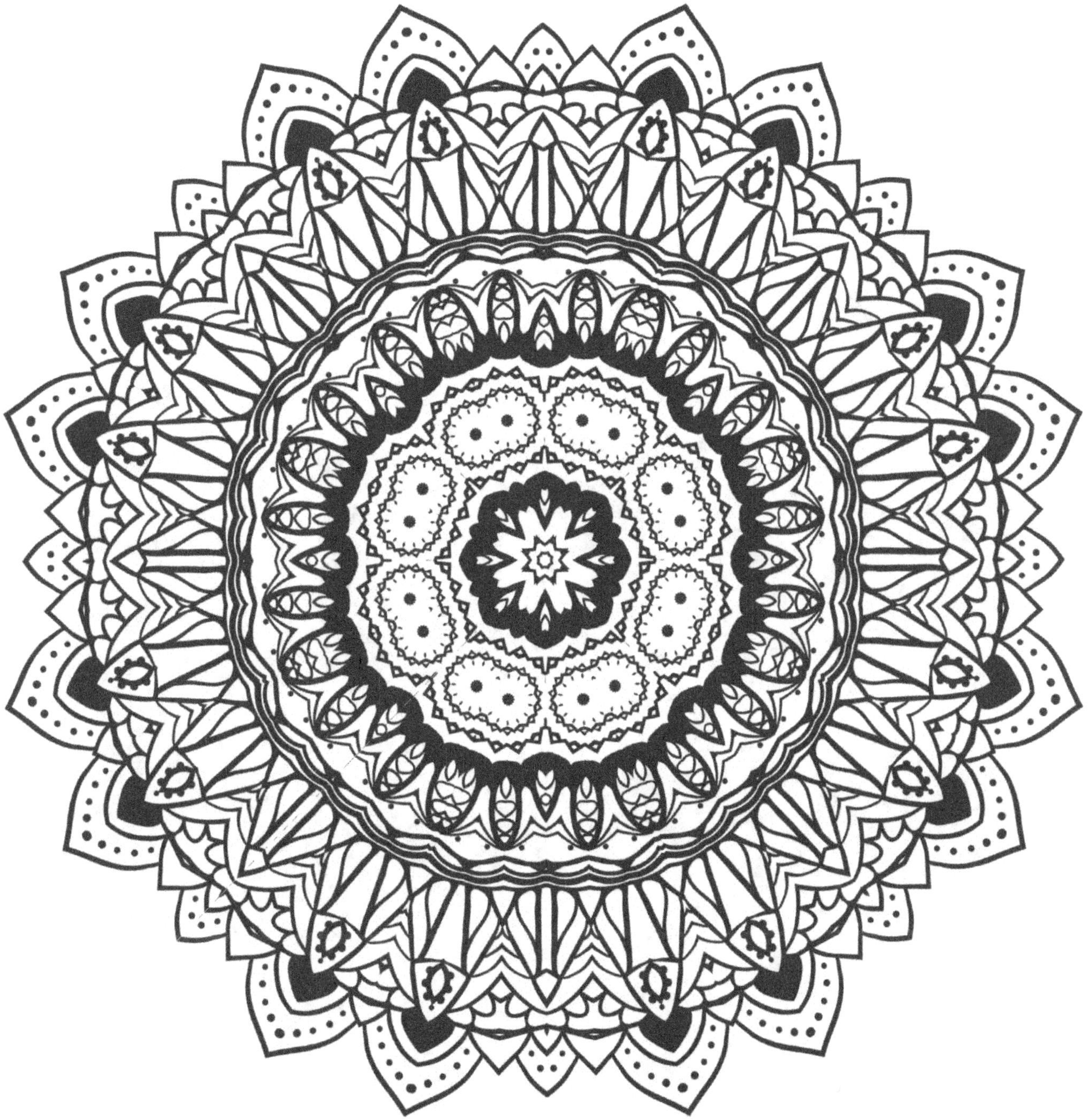

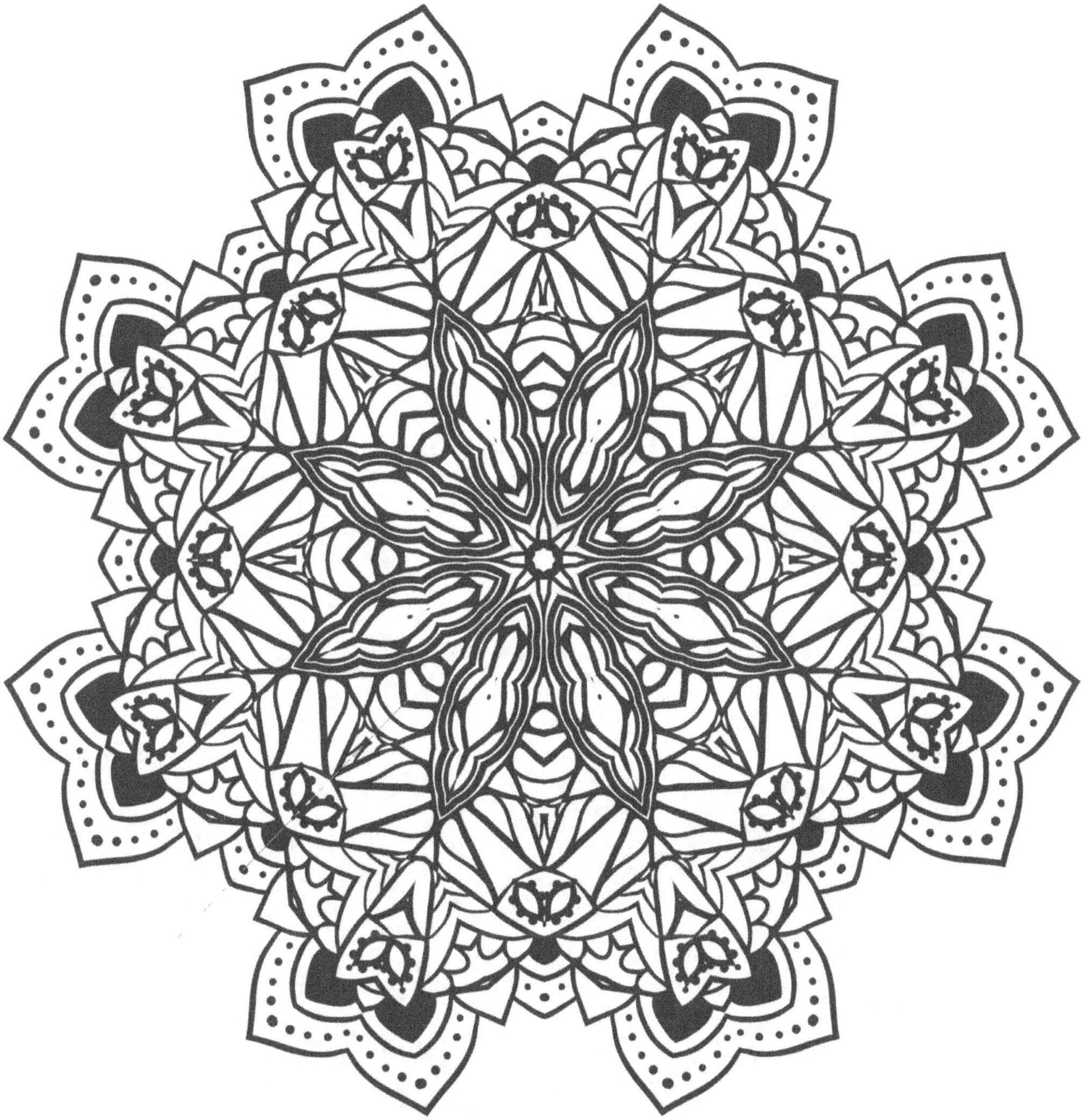

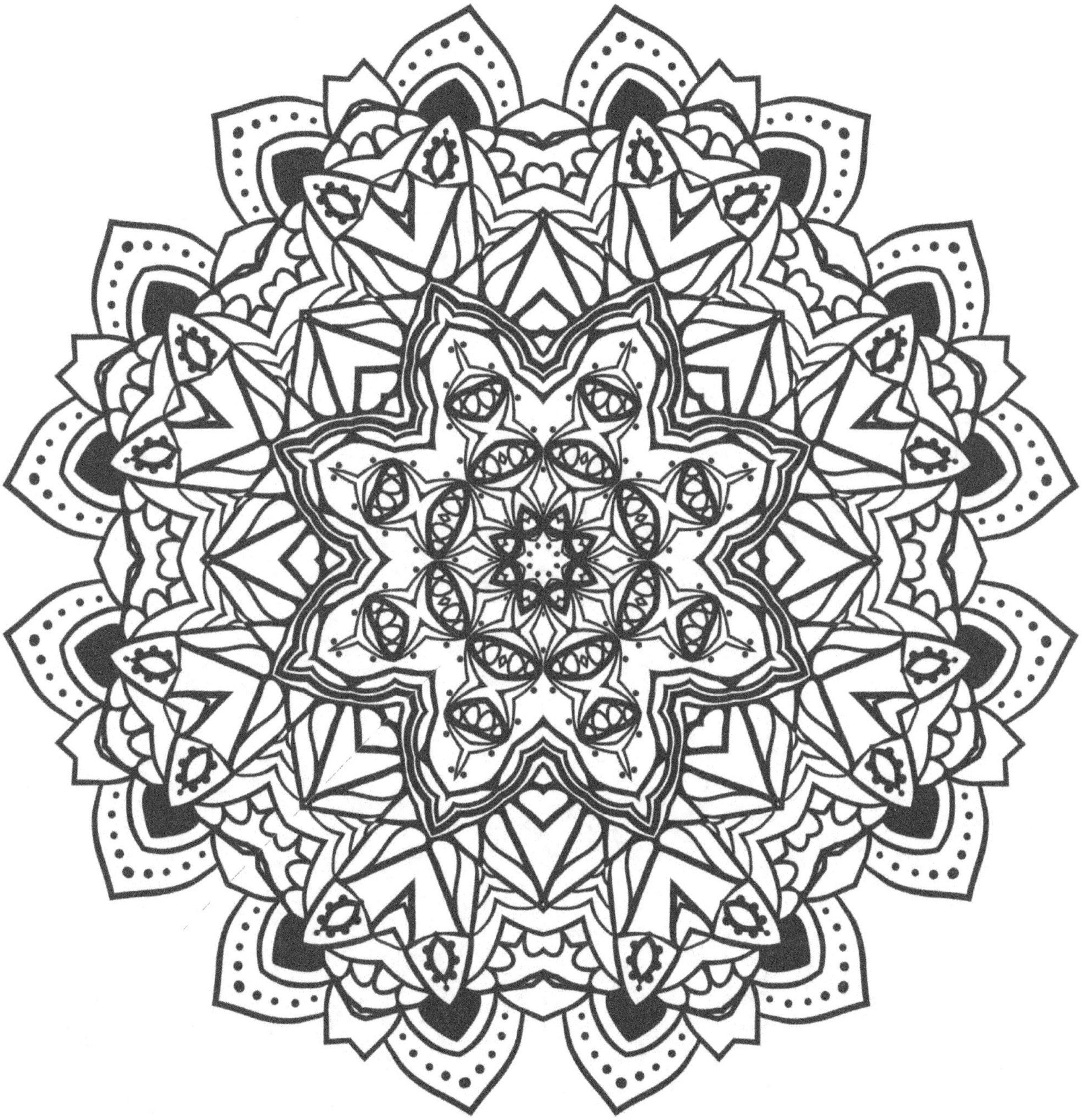

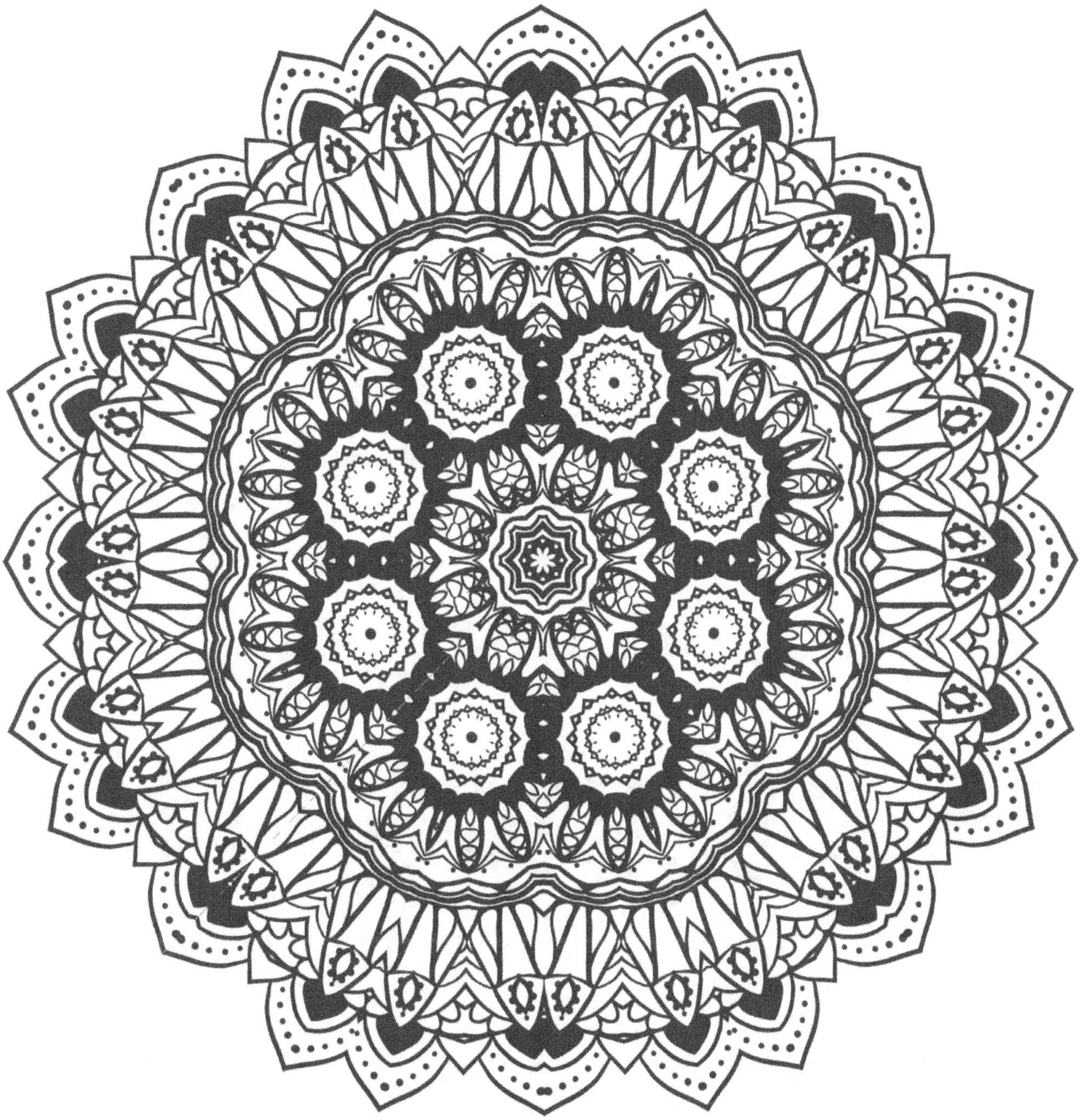

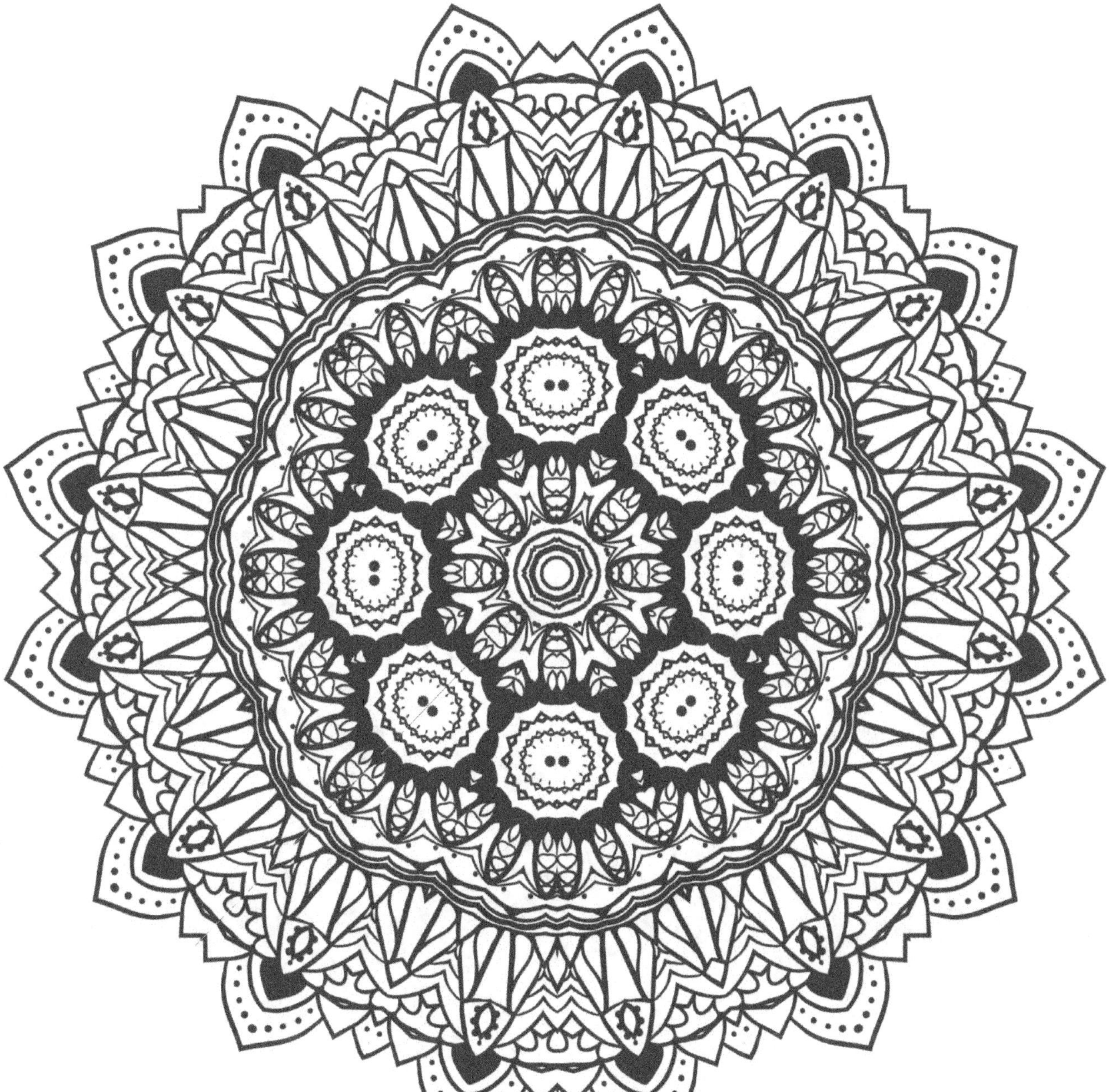

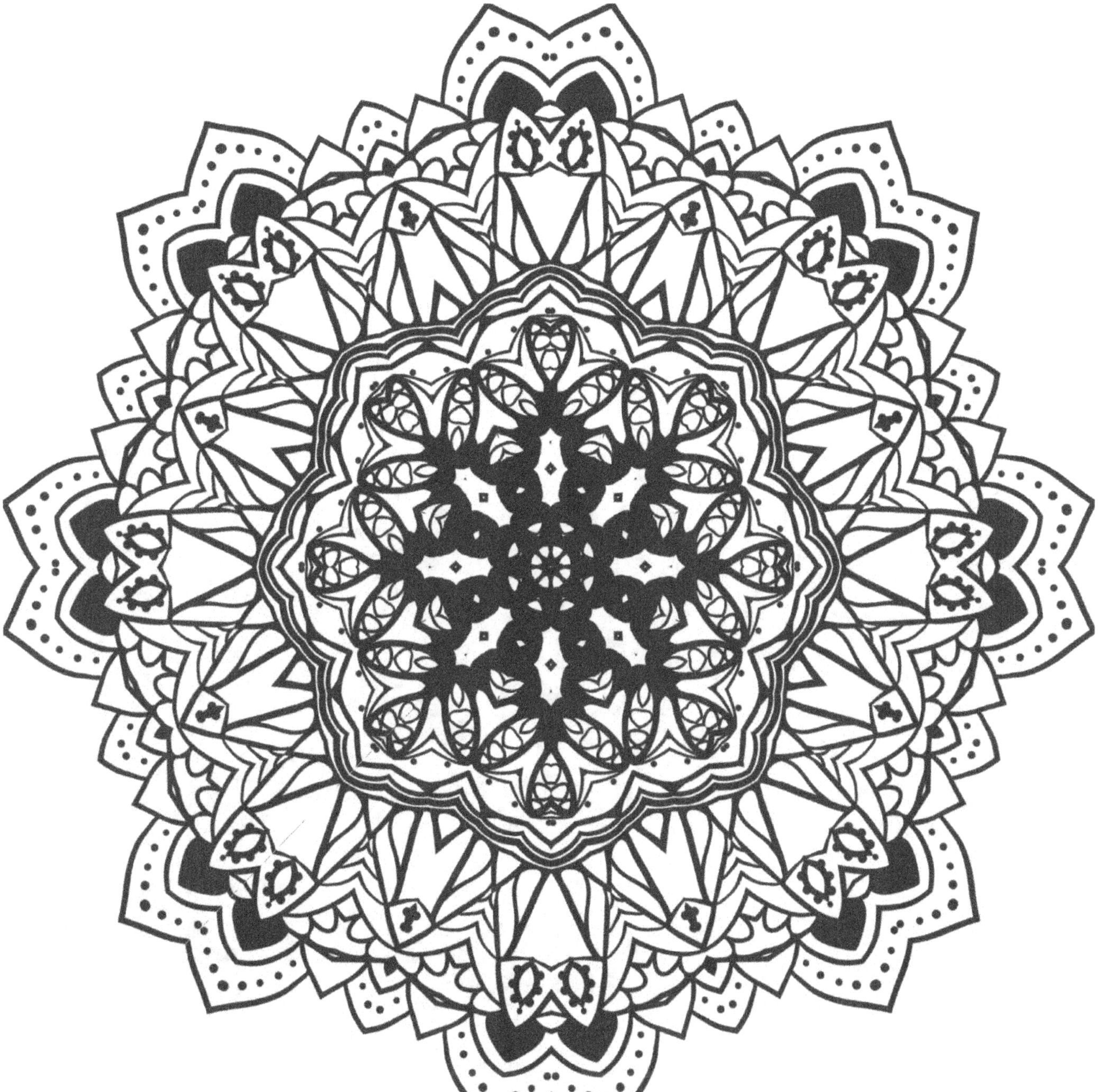

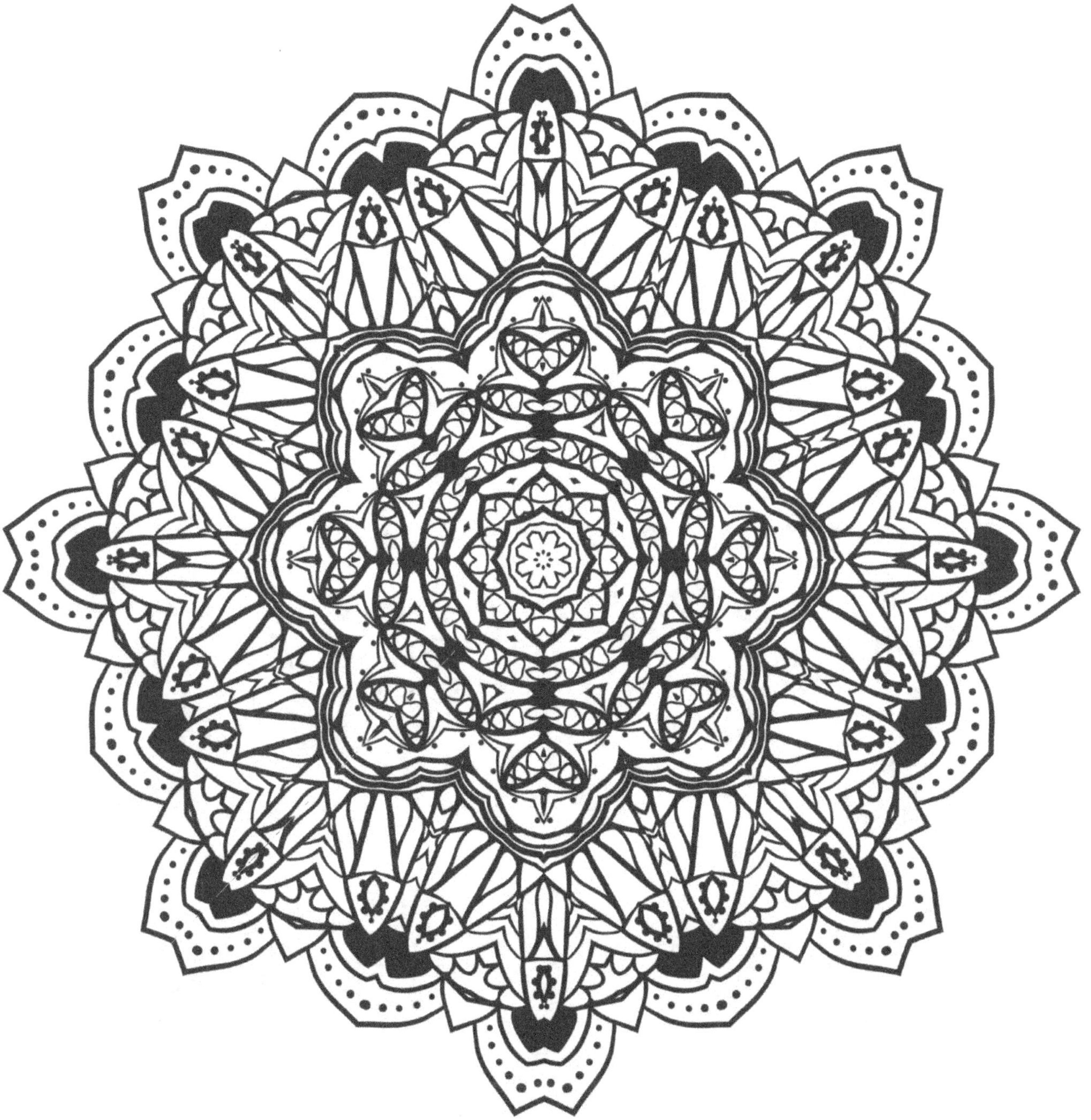

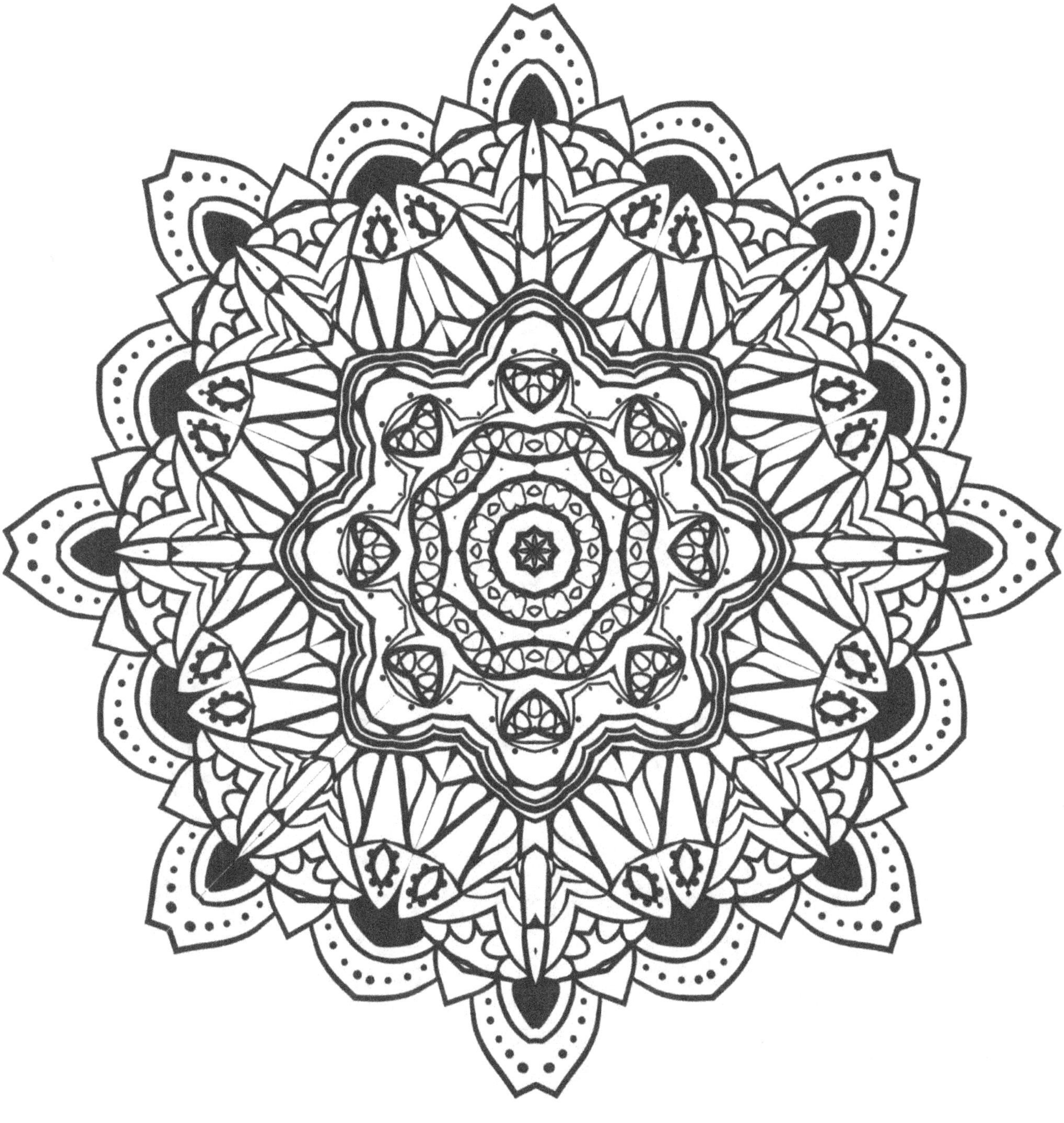

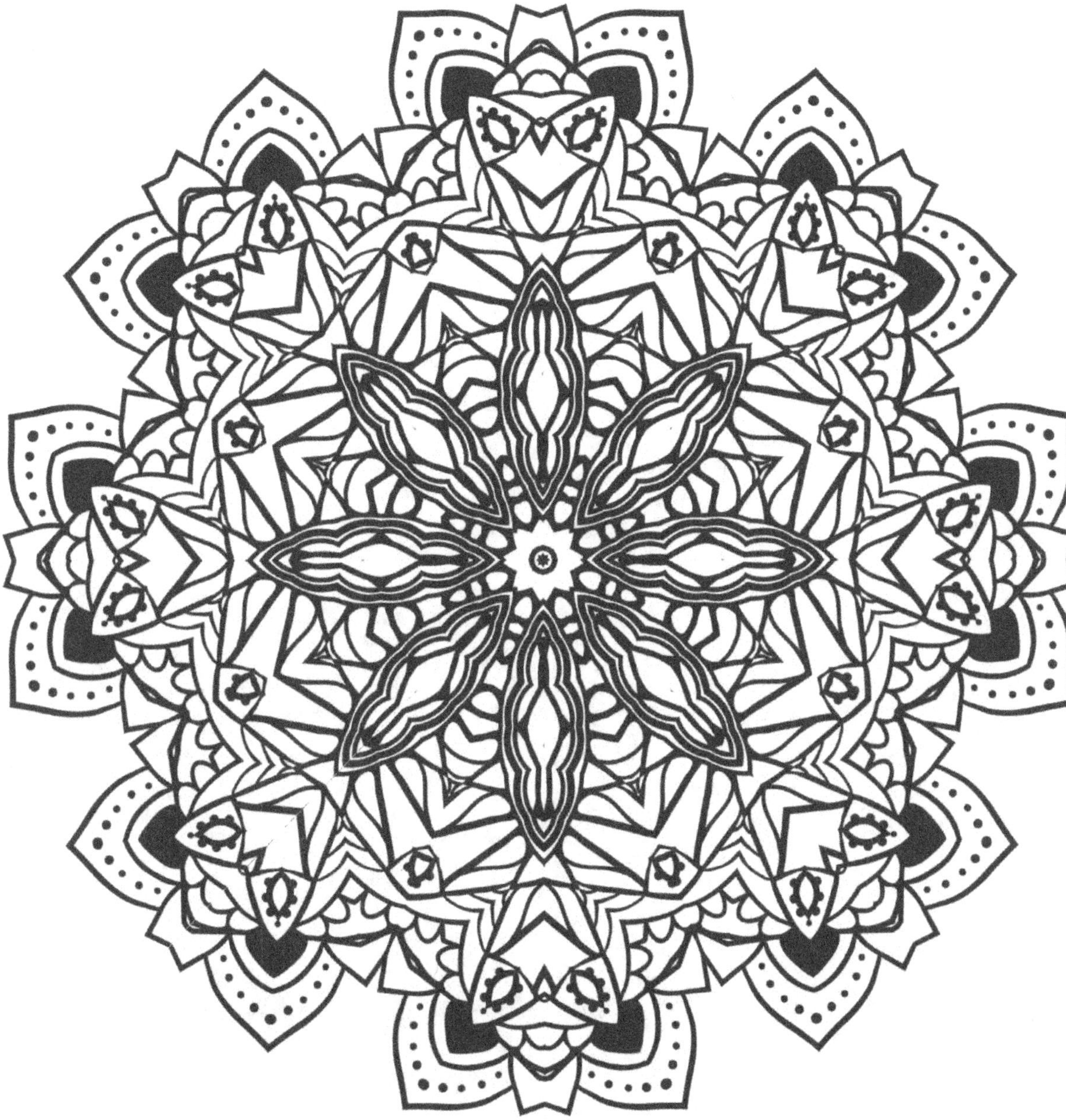

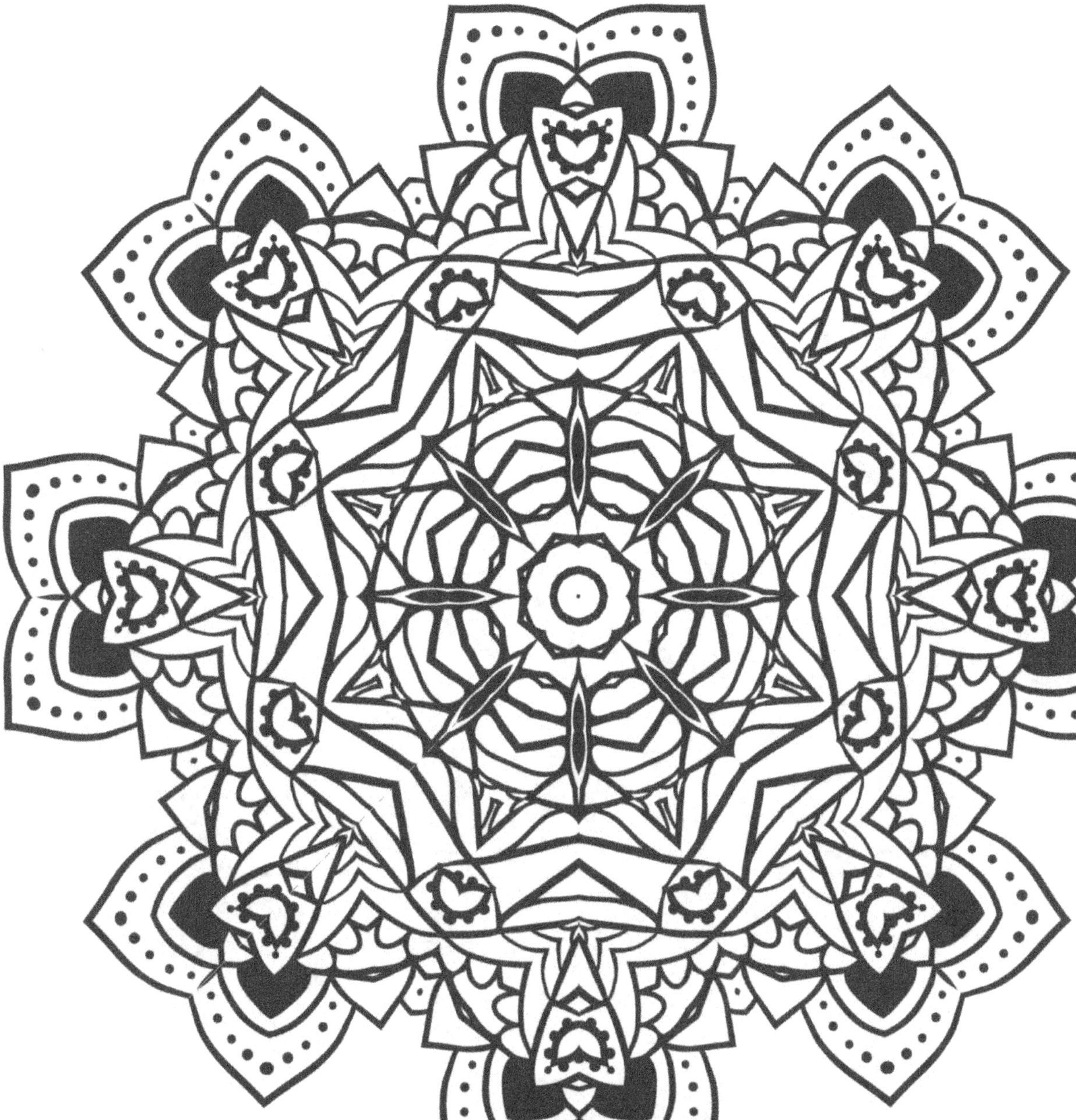

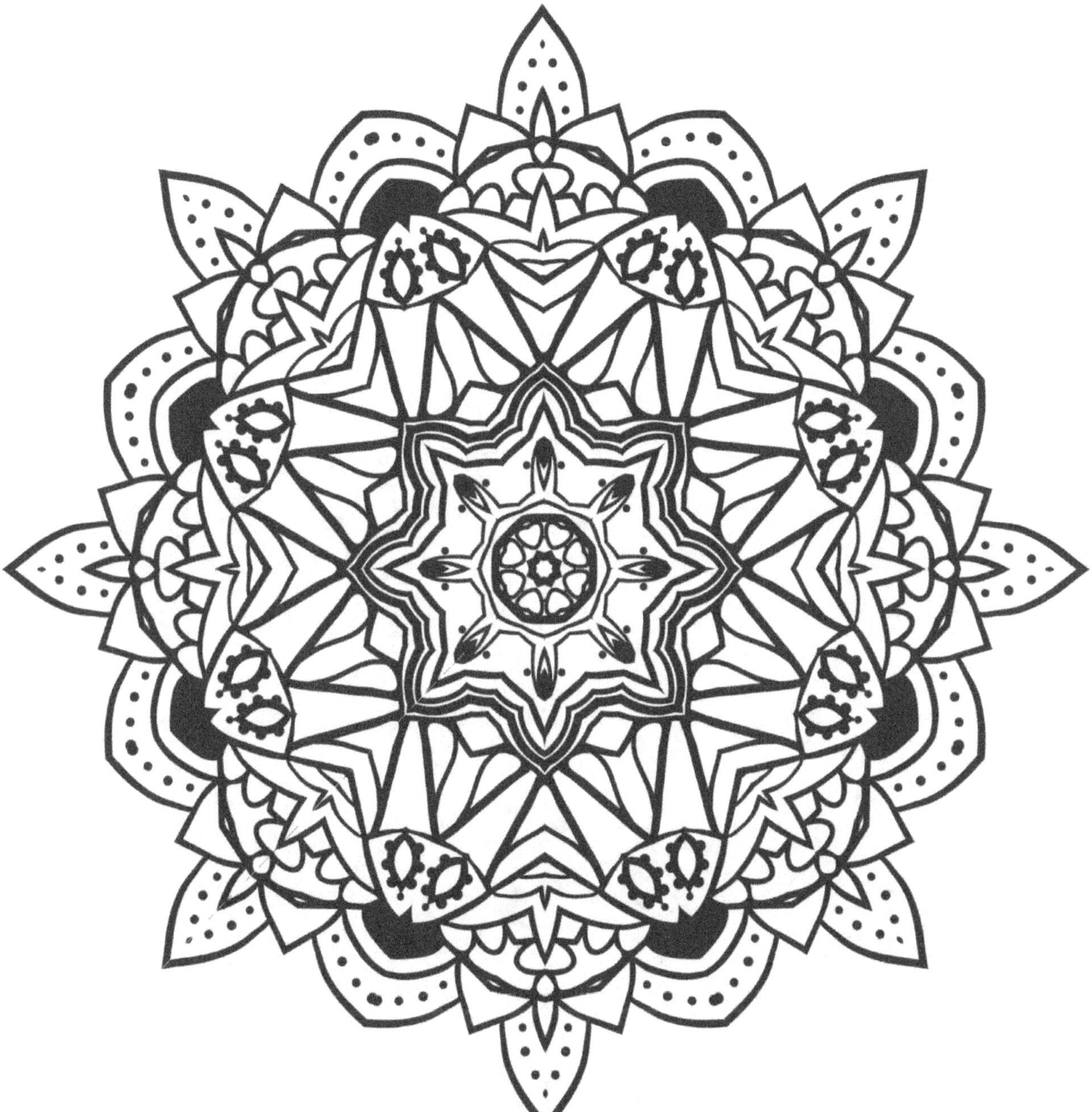

Hope you enjoy this coloring book.

Thank you.

www.ingramcontent.com/pod-product-compliance
Lightning Source LLC
Chambersburg PA
CBHW080834180526
45168CB00006B/2675
9781516917136